Podcasting at School

Kristin Fontichiaro

Foreword by Diane R. Chen

LIBRARIES
UNLIMITED
A Member of the Greenwood Publishing Group

Westport, Connecticut • London

Library of Congress Cataloging-in-Publication Data

Fontichiaro, Kristin.
  Podcasting at school / Kristin Fontichiaro.
  p. cm.
  Includes bibliographical references and index.
  ISBN 978-1-59158-587-9 (alk. paper)
  1. Internet in education. 2. Podcasting. I. Title.
LB1044.87.F66 2008
  371.33'44678—dc22   2007035040

British Library Cataloguing in Publication Data is available.

Library of Congress Catalog Card Number: 2007035040
ISBN: 978-1-59158-587-9

First published in 2008

Libraries Unlimited, 88 Post Road West, Westport, CT 06881
A Member of the Greenwood Publishing Group, Inc.
www.lu.com

Printed in the United States of America

The paper used in this book complies with the
Permanent Paper Standard issued by the National
Information Standards Organization (Z39.48–1984).

10 9 8 7 6 5 4 3 2 1

*For my father, an early adopter of educational technology,
and for the Beverly Podcasting Club.*

Contents

Foreword   ix

Acknowledgments   xi

Introduction   xiii

■ Part I Podcasting Basics

Chapter 1 Web 2.0 and Podcasting   3

Chapter 2 Ten Myths about Podcasting   13

Chapter 3 Equipment and Software   17

Chapter 4 Vocal Techniques and Strategies   29

Chapter 5 Recording a Simple Podcast   33

Chapter 6 Publishing and Distributing Podcasts   43

Chapter 7 Launching Podcasting in Your School   55

■ Part II Ideas for Teaching and Learning with Podcasting

Chapter 8 Great Podcasting Lessons   67

Chapter 9 Advertisements   87

Chapter 10 Audio Tours   97

Chapter 11 Mnemonic Raps   111

Chapter 12 Radio Broadcasts   119

Chapter 13 Radio Plays   129

Chapter 14 Oral History Projects   141

Glossary   155

Bibliography   159

Index   163

Foreword

Practical ideas with visionary purpose. Educators, including library information specialists, need leadership while incorporating new technologies to enhance learning. Kristin Fontichiaro provides a wide range of knowledge and in-depth techniques for all levels. Whether you are a beginning podcaster or an experienced developer needing curriculum ideas for integrating speech and writing into the curriculum, you will find the support you have been seeking.

Podcasting gives voice to the Internet. Along with many Web 2.0 technologies, podcasting allows users to interact with, respond to, and create content. Speaking is a more natural form of communicating knowledge and intention. Voice technologies break down barriers of communication. Vocal warm-ups provided in this text help extend podcasting beyond recordings to performances.

Kristin Fontichiaro's six-step process of developing podcasts allows the focus to be on creating content and sharing knowledge, rather than dwelling on how to use the technology. While basic techniques are provided, the success of this title comes from guiding the reader beyond simple activities to professional learning community exploration and growth.

To new developers, podcasting can seem elusive and nonintegral to education. Is this simply another technology that will be supplanted? Many educators have seized on early technology innovations only to find their curriculum integration tenuous. Podcasting provides a wider range of options for instructing and publishing. The listing of over 100 great podcasting lessons included in this title enables you to choose the best lesson for your students. Kristin Fontichiaro incorporates a sense of story and drama in voice with concrete language arts skills integration.

Educators need implementation support, including step-by-step directions to finding no-cost, low-cost, and more sophisticated technology. This title wrestles with the ramifications of long-range planning storage solutions, access, distribution, student privacy, parental involvement, and earning administrative support.

Is podcasting a trend, a fad, or a useful technique? Like telephones, televisions, and computers, the power in the technology lies in the usage by the consumer. Integrate podcasts into your lessons to give voice to learning.

Diane R. Chen

Acknowledgments

Thank you to my family for their patience, input, and editing expertise.

Many teaching and professional colleagues have collaborated and shared ideas with me, making this book possible. Thank you to Julie de Klerk, Marcia Mardis, Judy Hauser, Christine Knoper, Scott Levitt, Kim O'Rourke, Mary Beth Pardington, Ann Truesdell, Sue Taylor, Barbara Pepper, Vicki Pascaretti, Mike Iatrou, Kalyn Wulatin, Pat Boehm, Mikaela Bartoi, Teresa Sensenig, Roberta Sibley, Joyce Laszczak, Kurt Vogel, Kalyn Wulatin, and Deb Woodman. Several district leaders embraced this technology early on as a teaching and learning tool: Jennifer Martella, Barbara Jones Clark, Susan Hagner, Lisa Martinico, and Rob Glass. Thank you to Laurie Olmsted for suggesting the poetry contest podcast. Special gratitude goes to Jacquie Stephenson, former technology operations assistant at Beverly School, who was a sounding board for new ideas and technologies. Alec Barnes, Jacquie Stephenson, Mary Beth Pardington, and Laurie Olmsted gave feedback on the steps of the podcasting process. My thanks to the Beverly School staff and PTA for supporting our early podcasting experiments and to Best Buy for providing a TEACH grant for additional podcasting equipment.

A special thanks to the many Beverly School students who taught me how to better use podcasting in school, particularly the Friday Research Group and the Fourth Grade Podcasting Club.

Diane R. Chen, who writes the *Practically Paradise* blog for *School Library Journal*, shared the idea for taking a digital voice recorder to vendor booths at conferences. Her blog reflections on podcasting with cell phones provided a practical, free podcasting alternative.

Sharon Coatney, Debby LaBoon, Kelly Clifton, and Barbara Ittner of Libraries Unlimited envisioned this book before I did. Deborah Levitov of *School Library Media Activities Monthly* gave me many opportunities to write about Web 2.0 tools. Sue Kohfeldt, for this book as for the last, provided invaluable feedback. To Blanche Woolls, my mentor both here and as part of the American Professional Partnership for Lithuanian Education, I am deeply grateful.

Introduction

When I was in the first grade, my teacher set up a Califone cassette recorder in a dim corner of our classroom near the sink. At designated times, we students were allowed to enter the recording corner, push the "record" button, and speak into the recorder. The cassette recorder felt like a confessional, an intimate place for sharing information. We were able to express so much more through speaking than our nascent reading and writing selves could put on paper. We ended each recording by identifying ourselves: "This is Kristin Fontichiaro in Room 102." Later, parent volunteers would play back the cassette, typing our words on newsprint strips that we pasted to drawing paper and illustrated. Recording and publishing were intertwined.

When I first heard about podcasting, I was instantly transported back to first grade and those quiet moments by the sink. (At a recent gathering of childhood friends, I polled them: They had vivid memories of this experience as well,—and none of us had forgotten the room number of our first-grade teacher!) I realized that podcasting could do for my students what that Califone recorder did for me years ago. And when I tell this story to colleagues, I see the glow of recognition on their faces as they recall similar moments from their childhoods.

At its simplest level, podcasting takes away the cassette recorder and replaces it with a computer or other digital recording device (such as a digital voice recorder or an mp3 player equipped to make audio recordings). *Podcasting* is most commonly defined as the creation and distribution of a digital audio recording. Because the recording is digital, it can be duplicated, transmitted, and shared endlessly and quickly. Therefore, podcasting helps children reach out beyond their classrooms, sharing their learning with others in their schools, their neighborhoods, and their world.

When I began working with students to create podcasts in March 2006, we began with free software, $5 headsets (a headphone/microphone combination), and free online storage space. It was an instant hit. Our students and staff experimented with various techniques beyond radio shows. As our work grew, we collaborated with colleagues throughout the district, the county, the state, and the nation. The collaborative Podcasting at School wiki—(http://podcastingatschool. seedwiki.com)—served as a collective resource where information, best practices, and lessons learned could be shared. Any visitor to the Podcasting at School wiki is welcome to contribute feedback and ideas, creating an up-to-date resource that continues to enhance and complement the ideas in this book.

GOAL AND STRUCTURE OF THE BOOK

The goal of this book is to capture numerous techniques for integrating podcasts and podcasting into teaching and learning across the K–12 curriculum, from language arts to science, library orientations to social studies reenactments, foreign language practice to P.E. exercises. The book is written primarily for K–12 educators, though public librarians, community education leaders, troop leaders, and others who organize activities for children can easily adapt the concepts to fit their population's needs.

The book begins by clearly defining podcasting as one of many Web 2.0 tools, discussing the power of distribution, the impact on student learners, and dispelling of some podcasting myths. Next, the book discusses the practical "how-tos" of podcasting: software and hardware options, recording equipment, and free or inexpensive podcast hosting sites online. Practical file management strategies, including using iTunes to organize audio files, are also discussed. The book then explores a wide range of options for integrating instructor-made podcasts into the curriculum and for creating student podcasts. Some podcasting projects culminate by being posted online. However, the book also explores how podcasting tools can be used in less conventional ways. Clear, concrete instructions scaffold the instructional design of each activity.

ONLINE COMPANION TO THIS BOOK

The ideas in this book have developed both from my experience and from the contributed experiences of many other K–12 educators via this book's companion wiki, Podcasting at School (http://podcastingatschool.seedwiki.com). Anyone is welcome to add content to the wiki, either anonymously by clicking the "Edit" button, or by clicking "Create an Account," then "Login," to have changes credited to the writer.

CONCLUSION

Whether you are an experienced podcaster or just getting started, the ideas and concepts in this book can help you create instructionally relevant, intrinsically meaningful podcasts with students.

Part I
Podcasting Basics

Chapter 1
Web 2.0 and Podcasting

■ INTRODUCTION

Podcasting is known as a Web 2.0 tool, a product of the "read/write Web," in which the user becomes an active contributor of content to the Web. This chapter describes Web 2.0 and some of its components, defines podcasting as one of many Web 2.0 tools, discusses the value of podcasting at school, and provides an overview of the podcasting process.

■ WHAT IS WEB 2.0?

In the past few years, the term *Web 2.0* has been used to describe the current generation of the Internet. In the late twentieth and early twenty-first centuries, as the Internet had expanded into the homes of the majority of Americans, the Web was primarily a *static* environment. Web authors who knew how to write Web code using hypertext markup language (HTML) created content, and viewers visited their sites to read and view the content. Viewers were the consumers of content. Over time, however, new Web tools began to make it possible for anyone to create Web content for free, even without knowledge of HTML or other Web programming languages.

An early example of these no-cost, code-free tools is Geocities, now owned by Yahoo (http://www.yahoo.com/geocities), which provides free Web templates to users who register for a free Yahoo e-mail address. Free from having to design the "look" of a Web site or have the programming know-how to create and upload a page, sites like Geocities began to democratize the Web. Suddenly, anyone with access to the Internet—and by this point, most libraries offered Internet access for free—could publish online. Still, Web authors wrote the content, and visitors to their Web sites were merely passive viewers.

The success of Amazon.com (http://www.amazon.com) as the leading online bookseller brought about another example of the progression toward Web 2.0. Amazon.com began implementing features that allowed viewers to customize their visit. Customers were given tools that would let them contribute feedback on the site, including online wish lists, reviews, and reading lists. Suddenly, Amazon.com's content was not solely authored or shaped by Amazon.com staff; its customer base had become authors as well.

The Amazon.com customer experience helped to shepherd in the era of Web 2.0. *Web 2.0* is used to describe this "next generation" of Web content. It has been called the "read/write web," meaning that Internet visitors can not only read existing content, but also write and contribute content. Of all of Web 2.0's innovations, the three most ubiquitous in the K–12 arena are *blogs, wikis,* and *podcasts.* Each facilitates online publication by teachers and learners. Although this book focuses on podcasting, each of these media works in an interrelated way, so each is defined.

■ BLOGS

A blog is one of the major innovations of Web 2.0. Many people compare a blog to a journal kept online. Each new entry, called a "post," is automatically time- and date-stamped and posted online in reverse chronological order, so that the newest post appears at the top of the screen, the second newest below it, and so on. Millions of people keep personal or professional blogs for a variety of purposes.

Blogs have several benefits over Web pages. On a Web page, older content is often deleted to make room for new material. Blogs represent *accumulated* content, with older content always available via automatically generated archives.

Next, blogs can be easily configured to be *interactive.* They allow comments or feedback to be posted. Comments can be posted automatically or held in queue for the administrator to approve them before they appear. When a student's podcast is featured on a blog, his or her peers, family, and teachers can provide feedback and encouragement via comments. This helps students sense the real-world audience listening to their podcasts.

Blogs come with premade templates, so no Web design skills are necessary. They can be set up in less than 20 minutes. Most allow photographs to be uploaded to a post. Many educators remark that editing and use are easier with blogs than Web pages.

Finally, most blogs are free, making them perfect for educational use. Google's Blogger site (http://www.blogger.com) offers clean templates and interfaces with its Picasa photo editing software. A December 2006 upgrade allowed users to restrict the community that could access a blog by password-protecting them, making them a much more palatable option for educators. However, educators should examine the "Next Blog" button before choosing Blogger. This button, which appears on all Blogger pages, takes the user to a randomly selected blog, which might pose problems at the elementary level. Some workarounds for this are available. Try searching online using the terms *Blogger remove "next blog" button* for ideas. TypePad (http://www.typepad.com) is another favorite blogging option, although it requires a monthly fee.

A favorite option among educators is a blog built on the WordPress platform. WordPress is an open-source software, meaning it was created collaboratively by many users to benefit the greater good, not to generate profit. Many Web hosting companies now provide assistance in installing WordPress as part of a user's domain name (the author's professional blog, located at http://www.chiaroweb.com/blog, was set up this way). If this option is not available from a school's Web hosting provider, there are other options. One is to install WordPress manually on a Web site, which might require the assistance of technical services staff. The package can be downloaded from http://www.wordpress.org. Another is to use a free blogging host that provides free WordPress-based accounts. Free blogs are hosted by the WordPress consortium at http://www.wordpress.com.

Another great option is to use one of a series of blogging sites built on WordPress but provided specifically for educational use. Edublogs (http://www.edublogs.org) provides free WordPress blogs for educators. The author's school media center blog (http://beverlymedia.edublogs.org) is powered by Edublogs. Her media center Web page contains static, unchanging content. It then links to the blog for current events and student work. Learnerblogs for students (http://www.learnerblogs.org) and ESLblogs for English language learners (http://www.eslblogs.org) are other sites similar to Edublogs, though Edublogs has the greatest functionality.

Blogs have been used to capture learning in K–12 environments in a variety of ways:

- A high school humanities teacher requires students to submit discussion questions on a rotating basis throughout the semester. The teacher then posts them to his blog and gives the remaining students in the class a week to respond online. Because his Blogger site sends him an e-mail each time a comment is posted, he can easily credit students' work into his grade book.

- An elementary media specialist uses a blog to share student work with parents and document the activities of the media center.

- A school superintendent uses a blog to update the community on the status of budget reductions in the district.

- A principal uses a blog instead of the school's home page to record messages to parents. Because blogs automatically create archives, parents new to the school can read past postings to learn more about prior school activities.

- A classroom is working on reading and writing folktales. Working in teams, students post their work to a blog. Their classmates participate in peer review activities via the comments section.

- A foreign language teacher in the Midwest partners with a South American colleague for a pen pal program. Each classroom keeps a blog in his or her native language, posing questions. The students in the other classroom use the comments feature to reply to the questions, gaining practice with written language.

■ BLOGLINES, AGGREGATORS, AND RSS FEEDS

When blogs first launched, visitors had to seek them out. It could be frustrating as a reader to visit a blog only to discover that no new postings had been made. It could be equally frustrating to be the blog author, busily creating postings without readers being aware of them. It was like going to the newsstand each day to see if the latest magazine had come out yet: One might find it, or one might discover nothing.

Blogs were revolutionized by the introduction of RSS aggregators. *RSS* is commonly defined as "really simple syndication" or "real simple subscriptions." An *RSS aggregator* is a Web-based tool that lets readers have content from multiple blogs delivered to a single location, much as someone's magazine subscriptions are automatically delivered to a single mailbox. Through the aggregator, readers subscribe to their favorite blogs, and the aggregator checks those blogs automatically to look for new content. When new content is found, it shows up in the reader's aggregator, along with postings from all of the other blogs that the reader subscribed to. Now it is easy to keep up with dozens of blogs and postings.

For many educators, Bloglines (http://www.bloglines.com) is the RSS aggregator of choice. A free account, which collects no more personal information than the user's e-mail address and password, allows the user to subscribe to hundreds of blogs. Users can search the content of blogs already tracked by Bloglines, submit the special RSS code from a favorite blog of their choice, or even install a special button in Internet Explorer™ or Mozilla Firefox™ that automatically creates a Bloglines subscription when a user visits a promising blog. Google Reader (http://reader.google.com) is another popular RSS aggregator. Internet Explorer, Mozilla Firefox, and Microsoft Outlook also have built-in RSS tools.

■ WIKIS

Wikis are Web pages that can be authored or edited by multiple users. The word *wiki* comes from the Hawaiian expression "wiki wiki," or "quick, quick." Wikis are usually very stripped-down versions of Web pages, concentrating on text rather than fancy images or Web-powered tools.

Many sites now offer free wikis. Some of the wiki sites commonly used by educators are PBWiki (http://pbwiki.com), Seedwiki (http://seedwiki.com), and Wikispaces (http://www.wikispaces.com). In training sessions for educators and in use with elementary students, this author has discovered that Seedwiki is the simplest to use for newcomers.

Many wiki companies have levels of subscriptions. Basic wikis are often free, although additional features—such as the ability to password-protect the site or allow only selected users to contribute to edit content—may require a modest fee.

Wikis are best used to gather a variety of individuals' ideas, opinions, and edits in a single location. The outcome, known as *collective knowledge*, is stronger than any one person's contributions. The most ambitious wiki project to date is Wikipedia (http://en.wikipedia.org), which harnessed the power of "anyone can edit" to create the world's first free online encyclopedia. By opening up authorship to anyone (authorship rights have since been restricted), Wikipedia bet on the premise that a community of content creators would perpetuate a continual "checks and balances" system to ensure accuracy. Sometimes information of questionable taste or accuracy has gone unnoticed. Still, Wikipedia remains an extraordinary example of how the collective power of many can create a new, vibrant source of information.

Wikis' real power in the K–12 classroom is in gathering knowledge. Following are some examples of how wikis have been used in the K–12 environment:

- A school is creating its accreditation report. It posts the draft document on a password-protected wiki so that all committee members—from the principal to parents—can access, read, edit, and add to the material.

- During a Battle of the Books project, students collect their thoughts and perceptions on a wiki, creating a rich study guide prior to the event.

- A district uses a wiki as a central repository for technology tips and help sheets.

- While debating the stories for their weekly radio podcast, students use a wiki to keep track of the lineup.

- As an academic department prepares to attend a conference, it uses a wiki to track who will attend each session. They take notes during the sessions and post those notes to the wiki for those department members unable to attend.

The companion Web site for this book (http://podcastingatschool.seedwiki. com) is built on a wiki platform so that all readers of this book can pool their knowledge and experiences.

▮ PODCASTING

A *podcast* is a digitally created audio recording that is shared with others. The most common way to share a podcast is to post it online, then place a link to that file on a Web site, wiki, or blog.

Distribution is a key element of podcasting. Because podcasts are recorded digitally, they can be edited, merged, duplicated, distributed, and shared with a few mouse clicks. Often there is little or no cost associated with distribution. While many people hear *podcasting* and think that podcasts must be played on an iPod, the sleekly styled music player produced by Apple (http://www.apple. com/ipod), this is untrue. Especially in an educational environment, a variety of distribution and listening scenarios are useful.

■ THE PODCASTING PROCESS

As shown on page 9, there are six basic steps to creating a meaningful podcast in a school environment. These steps can be applied to all of the projects found in this book.

Step One: Picture It

In this step, the students or teacher decide on a topic or subject area focus for the podcast, as well as a desired purpose (e.g., to persuade or inform). Next, the audience is determined. Is this recording being made for parents? Peers? Older students? Younger students? Administrators? The larger community? Knowing the audience will help students make appropriate choices when crafting their recording. A recording genre is chosen, such as an interview, a radio advertisement, an informative broadcast, a public service announcement, a radio play, or a gallery tour. By envisioning the final product in advance, students are more likely to create products that are aligned with the teacher's intentions.

Step Two: Plan It

Whereas the picturing stage is a creative, visioning stage, the planning stage is more practical, as students set deadlines, outline the project, do research, write interview questions, and prepare for recording.

▶ Researching

When the project has been envisioned, research may be conducted if necessary. For example, if students are presenting a public service announcement about the importance of wearing seat belts, they will need to find and synthesize information about seat belt regulations and safety statistics. For a radio interview segment with a visiting author, they will need to know some of the author's work, his or her style, and something about his or her influences.

▶ Preparing Written Notes

While some podcasts can be made on the fly, without any prewriting or writing, student podcasts are most effective if they have a basic outline. This is modeled on the work of "real" radio and television personalities. Remind students that when they see news reporters or talk show hosts, those on-air personalities often are holding notebooks or small index cards or using teleprompters. Professionals want to do their best work, and they rely on notes to do it. Depending on the level of spontaneity desired for the project, the written notes can range from an outline to a list of questions to a fully written script.

▶ Rehearsing

Finally, students rehearse the basic steps of the podcast. They make sure they know how to operate the equipment, do a test recording to make sure the microphone will pick up their voices, and rehearse saying the words they have written.

When these steps are complete, students are ready to begin the recording process.

The Podcasting Process

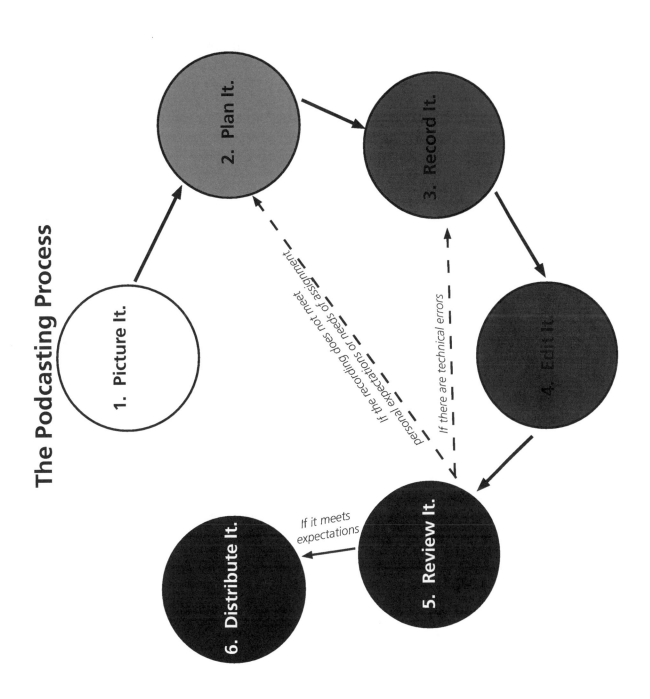

1. Picture It.

2. Plan It.

3. Record It.

4. Edit It.

5. Review It.

6. Distribute It.

If the recording does not meet personal expectations or needs of assignment

If there are technical errors

If it meets expectations

Step Three: Record It

With the planning step complete, the next step is to make the recording. Students begin by warming up their voices. Because the audience of a podcast cannot see the person speaking, they must rely on the speaker's vocal delivery to understand the content. Vocal warm-ups, described in more detail in Chapter 4, prepare the lips, teeth, tongue, and vocal cords to move flexibly to create clearly understood recordings.

Next, organize the recording area. If recording with a desktop or laptop computer, be sure that the mouse is within the reach of the user. Microphones should be placed in such a way that the user does not strain his or her neck area to speak into it. Scripts should be laid flat so they cannot rustle and create wind effects during recording.

Finally, make a test recording to set sound levels, then make a final recording.

Step Four: Edit It

Editing smoothes the rough edges of a recording. A few mouse clicks, and "um's, "ah's," and long pauses are removed. Interview questions can be rearranged. Sound effects and background music can be added.

Step Five: Review It

During this stage students review the work they have done so far. Using a rubric, discussion, or other self-evaluation tool, they check their work for technical quality and for content, possibly returning to an earlier phase in the process if needed, as shown on page 9.

Step Six: Distribute It

▶ *Exporting to mp3 Format*

Regardless of the software used to create a podcast, the software will first save the files in its own proprietary format. This allows many tracks to be "laid out" or positioned in the recording. Each track can be edited independently. For example, for a podcast with opening music, one voice, and a sound effect, each can be given its own track in the software so that each can be manipulated individually.

When editing is completed, the podcast must be *exported,* or converted, into a ubiquitous format that is understood by all computers, iPods, and mp3 players, regardless of the brand name or version of the device. The individual tracks are consolidated into a single track and can no longer be edited independently. The mp3 format is currently the most understood file format. Follow the software's instructions to convert the edited file into mp3 format.

▶ *Distribution*

The final act is to distribute and share the podcast in one of the following ways.

Listen to a podcast played on a computer.

- A teacher makes a podcast of himself as he dictates the words for a spelling test. When an absent child returns, she uses a computer in the classroom to play back the test while the teacher moves on with the rest of the class to the next lesson.

- A media specialist records her original variation of a classic fairy tale and designates a computer in her media center as a listening station for students who have completed their book checkout.

- A group of high school civics students conducts oral history interviews throughout the community. They host an evening open house, and guests are invited to move from computer to computer in a lab, listening to the interviews.

Transfer the podcast to an mp3 player or iPod.

- A special education student whose individualized education plan (IEP) mandates that tests be read aloud to him listens to a podcast of the test created by his paraprofessional.

- Students visiting an environmental center check out mp3 players from the center and wear them to hear an interpretive nature tour as they follow a trail in the woods.

Upload the podcast to the Web.

- During a research project, the teacher and media specialist use digital voice recorders to capture research conferences. They post these conversations onto the Web to help parents understand the cognitive and emotional processes of research and to assess the effectiveness of the instructional design.

- The podcasting club posts its weekly projects to share with family and classmates.

Create an RSS feed (into iTunes).

A *serial podcast* is an episode in a longer series of podcasts of related formats or themes, such as a weekly news broadcast. With a serial podcast, little context is necessary for the listener, as he or she is already familiar with the series' format. In the case of a serial podcast, a common form of distribution is to set up an account with iTunes (http://www.apple.com/itunes), which automatically retrieves the creator's newest podcasts, then to invite listeners to subscribe via iTunes.

- Ms. Smith's class creates a weekly radio show, with stories focusing on the week's curriculum topic. Parents and administrators can "tune in" by subscribing to the show in iTunes.

- Mr. Brown teaches calculus. The day before each test, he reviews the major concepts of the chapter with his class. He captures these review sessions as podcasts. His students subscribe via iTunes. When spring comes and they need to prepare for the Advanced Placement exam, students use the podcasts as study guides.

Send the podcast via e-mail.

- A teacher believes that a student may have a need that requires speech therapy and sends a sample audio file to a speech therapist who is not in residence in the building.

- A teacher records a lesson and e-mails it to a hospitalized child.

Burn the podcast to an audio CD.

- A class is motivated to write by a teacher and media specialist who encourage the students to be "rock star writers." The students choose their best work from their portfolios and record it onto a podcast. Gathering the podcasts into iTunes, the teacher and media specialist burn the files onto a CD. Students use adhesive labels to customize the CD, and the class invites parents and administrators to a launch party in celebration. A new CD is made each quarter. At the conclusion of the year, the teacher and media specialists use iTunes to resort the class's podcasts by artist's name (e.g., student's name) and burn an individual portfolio CD for each student. A copy is slipped into each student's permanent record.

- A local history class creates an audio tour of notable architecture. The tour is burned to a CD so that patrons can hear the narration on a driving tour.

■ CONCLUSION

Podcasting is one of a myriad of Web 2.0 tools that provide an innovative way to activate, motivate, and share students' learning and understandings. The next chapter debunks some of the perceived myths about podcasting.

Chapter 2
Ten Myths about Podcasting

■ INTRODUCTION

As I speak with other educators, I often hear "I can't," followed by a rationale for why podcasting is outside the grasp of their particular school or media center. Given the many ways in which podcasting can motivate students, reach out to aural learners, assist students with special needs, and share the classroom experience with parents and administrators, it is worthwhile to debunk these myths here.

Myth 1: I can't podcast because I don't have a budget for expensive software

There is a wide range of podcasting software, including some very good free software. GarageBand for Mac is a robust, full-featured audio recording program that ships free as part of new Mac computers. Audacity is a widely used open-source program that can be downloaded for free for Macs and PCs.

Myth 2: I can't podcast because I don't have new computers

The Audacity software is available for systems as old as Windows 98 or Mac OS9. Podcasting can also be done over the phone and automatically uploaded to the Web on your behalf (see Myth 4).

Myth 3: I can't podcast because I don't have iPods

Many people confuse podcasting and iPods. Podcasting software can be used to make projects that can be heard in many ways: on a desktop or laptop computer, via the Internet, burned to CD, *or* downloaded onto an iPod or other mp3 player. iPods are optional to the success of a podcasting project.

Myth 4: I can't podcast because my district won't allow us to add any software to our computers

Using a landline telephone or cell phone is an alternative to using a portable voice recorder or computer. Free or low-cost services such as Gcast.com or Gabcast.com are available that receive podcasts through a voice mail system. The user dials a telephone number, enters an identifying password via the keypad, then leaves a phone message. The service automatically converts the voice mail into an mp3 podcast and even hosts the file online for the user.

Myth 5: I'm not a techie—podcasting sounds too difficult for me to do

Most podcasting software has have a user interface that is similar to the buttons on a cassette recorder. Many mp3 players also have simple interfaces for recording a podcast. Finally, some podcasts are as simple as leaving a voice mail.

Myth 6: I can't podcast because my district's Web site doesn't permit the uploading of audio files

Some school districts have adopted content management system (CMS) templates that do not allow audio files to be uploaded. However, free podcast-hosting sites are available. Upload the file to one of these sites and link to it from your district Web page.

Myth 7: Podcasting is nothing more special than talking into a cassette recorder

On the contrary: Podcasting can be as simple as using a cassette recorder, but it is *much* more flexible and robust. Podcasting allows student work to be easily edited, removing errors and adding sound effects and music. More important, podcasting makes digital files that can be transmitted and shared easily. Students, knowing their work has a real-world audience, gain motivation to do quality work.

Myth 8: Podcasting is just a fad

It is possible that podcasting will someday go the way of the pet rock and rainbow suspenders. However, given that podcasting has been adopted by amateurs and professionals alike, from *60 Minutes* to National Public Radio, it is unlikely that podcasting will disappear entirely. (Think of the first time you heard about e-mail . . . or a cell phone . . . many thought they were fads, too!)

Myth 9: I can't podcast because my curriculum emphasizes writing over speaking

Many states now have state-level writing assessments. Podcasting can complement the writing process, not supplant it. While some podcasts have improvised content, most projects rely on the writing and publishing process to prepare student work for broadcast. Podcasting can even be used during the editing process. Many elementary-age students become better proofreaders when they read the draft of a piece of writing into a podcasting microphone. As they read, they stumble over their mistakes and discover awkwardly worded phrases. Podcasting can be a partner in the writing process, not a substitute for it.

Myth 10: I don't podcast because it endangers student privacy

Student privacy can be protected in several ways. Avoid giving the student's last name or assigning projects that ask students to reveal personal details such as sibling names, home address, or church or sports affiliations. Or let students use their class numbers or give themselves a fun nickname or nom de plume. With a bit of advance planning, students can be safe when uploading podcasts to the Web.

CONCLUSION

There really are no barriers to bringing podcasting into school.

Chapter 3
Equipment and Software

■ INTRODUCTION

This chapter summarizes the dizzying variety of podcasting recording options. These options can be generalized into three main categories: using software to record directly onto a computer, using a portable device for recording, and calling a telephone number to leave a voice mail that is later converted to a podcast. Costs range from free to hundreds of dollars.

■ RECORDING DIRECTLY ONTO A COMPUTER

There are two requirements for recording a podcast with a desktop or laptop computer: a microphone and software.

Headsets

A headset combines a set of headphones with a small microphone that is placed approximately one to two inches from the mouth. Headsets have two plugs, which connect to the computer's ⅛-inch headphone and microphone jacks. Students can easily replay their work through the headphones without disturbing others. Because the microphone picks up only close sounds, it blocks much of the background noise in noisy classrooms or computer labs. If considering purchasing headsets for podcasting with a desktop computer, be sure that the headset cord is long enough to reach from the back of the desktop, where the jack may be located. Students should be able to move their heads or even stand up without pulling the cord taut. While some microphones come with foam mouthpieces to help mute the sound of *plosives* (phonetic sounds like "p" and "b" that push air out of the mouth), microphones without foam may be preferable for the school environment because they can more easily be cleaned with sanitizing wipes. These headsets will come with two color-coded plugs, one (generally red or pink) that is inserted in the microphone jack, and another (often green or black) that is inserted in the headphone jack. A mnemonic device for remembering which plug belongs with which jack is to remember that lips, which speak, are pink or red, so the red or pink plug goes in the microphone jack.

Recommended for schools because of its inexpensive cost (around $5), lack of foam mouthpiece, and general effectiveness is the AV-44 model manufactured by Avid (http://travelwithavid.com/headsets.html).

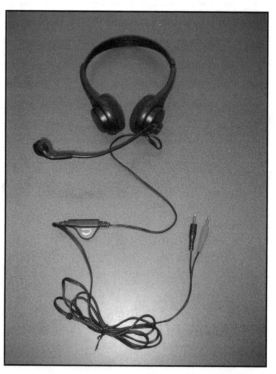

This inexpensive headset by Avid makes crisp, clear recordings.

A single headset will work for a solo podcast, but often podcasts are collaborative projects requiring more than one participant. Although a computer will have only one microphone and headphone jack, a series of "Y" adapters can enable up to four headsets to be connected to a single machine.

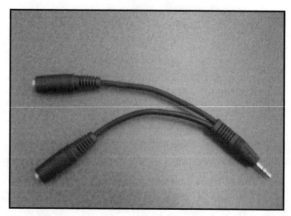

A "Y" adapter can be purchased at a stereo store. Purchase two for each computer: one for the microphone input and one for the headphone jack.

A "Y" adapter, so named because it is shaped like a "Y", has a single ⅛-inch plug on one end and two jacks on the other. For a two-person interview, two "Y" adapters will be needed, one to join the two microphones together and one to join the two headphones together. For a three- or four-person project, four "Y" adapters will be needed. There is virtually no reduction in sound quality for up to four headsets ganged together with "Y" adapters.

These adapters can be purchased for approximately $6 each at a stereo supply store such as Radio Shack. If these adapters will be loaned out, consider bar coding them and checking them out via the school library media center.

Microphones

Many laptop computers now have microphones built into the case of the computer. In some computers, such as the laptops manufactured by Apple, the sound quality of the internal microphone is remarkably good. However, having an external microphone is generally preferred, as it can generate a higher quality of sound and better discriminate between intentional sound and unwanted background noise.

There are many varieties of podcasting microphones for professional use, but this book focuses on inexpensive microphone options to permit scalability and replicability of podcasting projects throughout a school or district.

Microphones are available for computer use with two types of connections. The first is a ⅛-inch jack that plugs into the microphone jack of a computer (marked with the icon of a 1940s-looking microphone on a stand). This type of jack is generally found on some Macintosh models and almost all PC computers. The second type connects to the computer via a USB port. Macintosh laptops that lack dedicated microphone jacks must use a USB microphone. PC computers are often confused if users try to combine a ⅛-inch microphone with a USB microphone, so an either/or approach is recommended.

The $30 Logitech USB Desktop Microphone, model #980186-0403 (http://www.logitech.com), is an inexpensive model with decent sound quality and is available from many major retailers. Blue Mic's Snowball microphone, at just under $100 (http://www.bluemic.com) is a splurge but effective for placing in the middle of a classroom or conference table, as it can pick up large amounts of ambient sound.

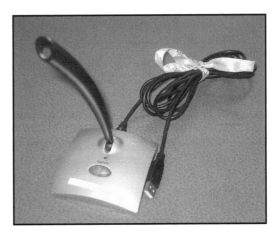

This Logitech USB microphone is appropriate for computers that lack standard microphone jacks or for recording sound effects.

USB microphones often come with a stand, making them good options for capturing sound effects for podcasts of fictional works, such as a radio play or a "live" report from a moment in history or literature (see Chapter 12, "Radio Broadcasts").

■ SOFTWARE

While microphones capture the sound, it is the software that records it, edits it, enhances it with special and sound effects, and packages it. Most software used for podcasting was actually designed for more sophisticated use, such as recording bands and musical ensembles, though it is anticipated that as podcasting gains in popularity, more podcasting-specific software will be released.

As with microphones, when choosing software schools must settle on a balance between quantity and features. Free software such as Audacity is scalable and easily expandable throughout an entire district, while investing more in a paid software might yield premium features such as a more appealing graphical interface, built-in *audio loops* (short, repeatable clips of music or rhythms that can be strung together to create background rhythms and beats or used for theme music) for theme music, or sound effects. Other considerations when selecting software are the types of software the school district has already determined that it will install and support and the minimum operating requirements required by the software.

GarageBand

GarageBand (http://www.apple.com/ilife/garageband/), which ships free with new Macintosh computers as part of the multimedia iLife software suite, in many ways represents the gold standard. It has an impressive library of audio loops, rhythms, and sound effects; and interfaces effortlessly with other iLife software products. The interface is intuitive and makes it easy to edit tracks together. GarageBand also facilitates the creation of enhanced podcasts, in which still images are displayed at specific points during the podcast. Enhanced podcasts have not reached the mainstream yet, however, as some fear they are little more than miniature PowerPoint™ slides with audio (but without the animations). Enhanced podcasts are not covered in this book. Also, because it works only with the Mac operating system, GarageBand is not a practical option for the many school districts running on a PC platform.

Audacity

Audacity (http://audacity.sourceforge.net) is the model software used throughout this book. It is free, open-source software. *Open source* means that the behind-the-scenes software coding is publicly available to software engineers and enthusiasts, who are invited to improve and enhance it. Audacity is appealing for school-based podcasts not only because it is free, but because it is flexible. There are versions available for both the Mac and Windows platforms. Machines as far back as Windows 98 are compatible, and legacy Mac users as far back as OS9 will also find a version for them.

Audacity has a user-friendly graphical interface, featuring a button-based top toolbar that mimics the buttons on a cassette recorder or CD player, making it easy for even the youngest students to make a basic recording. In addition, it has a series of special effects. A particularly nice feature of Audacity is that the volume of each individual track can be adjusted, making it easier to balance quiet performers with louder ones. Audacity also allows a variety of audio formats to be imported for editing. Audacity lacks the built-in audio loops and some of the visual flair of GarageBand. However, it has been embraced by many of the universities sponsoring major podcasting initiatives among their professors. Before spending money on any software, try Audacity.

Tool Factory Podcasting

Tool Factory Podcasting (http://www.toolfactory.com/products/page?id= 2121) is a relative newcomer to the podcasting market, and it is designed with K–12 users in mind. At $99 per license, it is more expensive, but one clever feature is that it combines scriptwriting and recording in a single program. The script is color-coded, making it easy for each student to find his or her place, and the sound waves created are also color-coded, making editing easier. Tool Factory Podcasting has some built-in sound effects, though they lack some of the professional quality of GarageBand. A free 30-day download is available.

QuickTime Pro

QuickTime Pro is a $49 addition to the free QuickTime video viewing software manufactured by Apple (http://www.apple.com/quicktime). QuickTime Pro offers one-button podcasting: that is, to begin recording, push a single button icon. Push it again to stop it. Due to its extraordinarily simple interface, QuickTime Pro is recommended for primary classrooms with very young users. However, it does not offer editing capabilities, limiting its use for older students and more complex projects. QuickTime Pro's best feature has nothing to do with podcasting: It can take existing QuickTime files and make them editable again in iMovie. If that feature is useful, consider QuickTime Pro. If not, other software is more fully featured and robust.

Acid Music Studio by Sony

Sony's Acid Music Studio (http://www.sonycreativesoftware.com/products/ acidfamily.asp) is a robust PC equivalent to Apple's GarageBand, with a highly complex interface. Musicians use Acid Music Studio to record their bands' compositions. Rich with audio loops, Sony Acid Music studio offers more musical sophistication at the user's finger tips. Users are invited to post their final projects on AcidPlanet.com, where competitions are ongoing. An appeal of Acid Music Studio is its free 30-day trial, which gives educators a chance to test run before purchasing. However, given its retail price of $59.95, it may be better suited for small groups, as it is an expensive undertaking at the building or district integration level.

Skype with Recording Software

At first glance, Skype (http://www.skype.com) seems like an unlikely choice for podcasting, its primary function is to facilitate Internet phone calls between computers with high-speed Internet connections, similar to other Voice over Internet Protocol (VoIP) endeavors. With free registration, users download a small piece of software that functions like a digital phone when partnered with a headset. The Avid headset discussed earlier in this chapter works well with Skype.

If users on both ends use Skype-enabled computers to communicate, the call is free. Skype also permits its users to use its connections to dial landlines or cell phones for a small fee. Skype's conferencing feature allows free multi-user conference calls between computers.

While Skype on its own can help students connect with experts around the world without taxing the district's telephone budget and is similarly useful for exchange students to make free calls home, when partnered with inexpensive recording software like HotRecorder™ (http://www.hotrecorder.com) or the free Powergramo (http://www.powergramo.com), Skype calls can be turned into podcasts. Simply begin the Skype call, then launch Hot Recorder to begin recording the conversation. Or start Powergramo, then initiate the Skype call (Nesbitt 2007). Be sure to request permission from the person being called prior to recording.

Skype plus one of these programs makes long-distance podcasts a snap. Want to podcast an interview with a Smithsonian expert without leaving Michigan's Upper Peninsula? Consult with Kenyan herding experts without leaving school? Host an inexpensive professional development question-and-answer session with a noted expert without paying expensive hotel and transportation fees? This exciting technology can help bring the global community to your students. For more details on using Powergramo with Skype, see http://www.geeks.com/techtips/2007/techtips-22feb07.htm (Nesbitt 2007).

■ PORTABLE AUDIO RECORDERS

Portability can unlock a whole new world of podcasting opportunities, as it takes podcasting to wherever the learning is happening. Recordings can be made in the cafeteria, on the playground, on a field trip, or in the hallway. Portable devices are small enough to be carried in an instructor's pocket in case a spur-of-the-moment teaching opportunity arises. Following are some examples of how a portable recording device can benefit a school community:

- The enrichment teacher has just revealed the top-secret titles for Battle of the Books. As students line up to check out, the media specialist moves among them and records students' enthusiastic first impressions. The enrichment teacher's perspective is also recorded. By the time the students get home with the permission slip for their parents, the podcast is already online, building student and family excitement for the program.

- A chemistry class is conducting an experiment. Each group has made a hypothesis about the results of the experiment. The chemistry teacher moves among the class as they work, interviewing students and asking them to compare their original projections with the actual results. On her way home from school, the teacher listens to the recording to identify gaps in understanding.

- The school social worker has organized Mix-It-Up Day, on which student seating assignments in the cafeteria are reorganized so that students sit with new colleagues and break diversity barriers. A student interviewing team roams the cafeteria to get student and faculty feedback.

- The fourth grade is visiting the state Capitol and will meet their state representative. Two students selected by lottery have prepared interview questions for their elected official and interview her immediately following the class photograph on the Capitol steps.

- A student group is traveling to Mexico for a service learning project during a school holiday. Armed with a series of portable recorders, they gather audio footage of colloquial Spanish for later use in the foreign language department, keep an audio diary of their experiences, and interview community service leaders to prepare a public service announcement for their hometown radio station.

Portable audio recorders are also useful in the classroom setting if few or no computers are available in the classroom. They can take the form of mp3 players or digital voice recorders.

Mp3 Players

In their earlier versions, mp3 players were considered to be primarily music players. However, many mp3 players now carry built-in audio recorders. Some "no-name" mp3 players can be purchased for as little as $15 online.

▶ *Video iPod or Second Generation iPod Nano with a Microphone Attachment*

For ease of use, elegance of design, and sheer "wow" factor, it is hard to beat the iPod line of products for recordings. While they do not have built-in recording devices, both the video iPod and the redesigned iPod Nanos have docking ports on the bottom that permit the addition of an external stereo microphone. Two high-quality accessories permit stereo-quality sound. One is the Belkin TuneTalk, which retails for approximately $70 (http://catalog.belkin.com/IWCatProductPage. process?Product_Id=277661). Two angled input microphones capture sound in stereo quality. Stereo sound may sound like an extravagance for voice podcasts, and, indeed, it does generate extremely large file sizes (it is best to upload the file into Audacity and export it from there to reduce the file size by up to 20 times), but its real use comes in recording sounds. For example, the TuneTalk can record choir practice, capture all the voices in a Spanish classroom, or capture the ambient sound at a zoo visit. An "autogain" button at the bottom of the TuneTalk helps to regulate sound, automatically boosting sound that is closer rather than farther away. However, in crowded situations, it is useful to hold the microphone approximately five inches away from the speaker's mouth. A benefit of the TuneTalk is that it can accommodate a hard case being placed between it and the iPod, protecting the iPod from accidental spills, drops, and breakage.

Similar external microphones for the video iPod include the Griffin iTalk Pro (http://www.griffintechnology.com/products/italkpro/) and the XtremeMac MicroMemo Digital Voice Recorder (http://www.xtrememac.com).

Older models of the iPod, including pre-October 2006 iPod Nanos, may be able to use a microphone input device that plugs into the headphone jack. Some older iPods can be "hacked" to convert an earbud into a microphone. Searching online using the search terms *iPod convert earbud microphone* for instructions. iPods are remarkably ubiquitous across socioeconomic lines; consider asking the local community to donate used equipment for this project.

Because iPods are configured to work with iTunes, the recorded files, known by Apple as "voice memos," are automatically transferred to the desktop computer when the device is synced. The files will automatically appear as audio files in the WAV format. WAV files can be read and played by the iTunes interface, and they can also be imported into Audacity for further editing. To find a WAV file that has been synced into iTunes on a PC, go into MY DOCUMENTS, then into the MY MUSIC folder, then ITUNES, then ITUNES MUSIC, and the file will appear, named with the date and time of the recording. Once the iPod with voice memos has synced with iTunes, the voice memos move location on the iPod and can be found under MUSIC > VOICE MEMOS.

Some versions of iTunes can be configured to automatically convert all incoming files into mp3 format. One minute of high-quality stereo recording can create a file as large as 10MB, which can bog down even fast Internet connections. While this saves time, these stereo-quality files may be large and unwieldy. If the recording is two or three minutes long, a large file size will not be problematic. In its recording window, the iPod can be set to record at high- or low-quality sound. If space allows, record in the highest quality format, then compress the files in Audacity.

In the educational arena, there are a few caveats about iPods. One is that iPod products are designed to sync with one computer's iTunes. If the user is a classroom teacher who will always use the same computer for transferring files, this will not be a problem. However, if the iPod will be shared among many teachers, it can be inconvenient to have a single computer for transferring files. Another is that the microphones attach externally and could break off if dropped. Finally, both iPods and their external microphones charge their batteries through the synchronization cable. If an iPod or its microphone loses power during a field trip, the batteries cannot be recharged when away from a computer.

▶ *Creative Zen Vision M*

An mp3 player comparable to the video iPod is the Creative Zen Vision M (http://www.creative.com/products/mp3/zenvisionm/). Starting at around $200, the player itself is less expensive than the video iPod, though it is not compatible with the popular iTunes or iTunes Store. One advantage, however, is that it has a built-in mono microphone (not stereo). Given that one could buy three Vision M players for the price of two video iPods with recording accessories, one may be willing to sacrifice stereo quality for price. An additional appeal for educators is that there is no external accessory that could break off if jarred.

Digital Voice Recorders

It seems that no business professional of the 1980s was complete without a minicassette recorder, a slender, palm-sized device that recorded dictation and audio memos. This device has been brought into the digital age, and audio files are now recorded onto internal flash memory. These devices, if used solely for podcasting, can be a better investment than a high-end mp3 player, as many useful models are available for under $100. One advantage of digital audio recorders is that they often have built-in speakers, allowing students to instantly review their work without having to carry headphones. The built-in speaker is often of quite poor quality; the recording may sound better once downloaded to a computer.

For some educators, a simple digital audio recorder that cannot play music, tune into the radio, or play a video, may be an appealing option. Stripped of these distracting features, digital voice recorders help keep students focused on the learning task. It may be useful to consider purchasing one that is compatible with voice-to-text translation software such as Dragon Naturally Speaking™ (DNS). DNS can be a tremendous boost for students who struggle with written expression, allowing them to dictate their work with remarkable accuracy. Users register the software and read a sample text aloud so that the software learns to recognize their unique vocal patterns. To find out if a digital voice recorder is recommended by DNS, visit its Web site at http://www.nuance.com/ naturallyspeaking. Even if a school does not plan to use DNS in combination with the player, the DNS recommendations can help in the identification of a recorder that provides a crisp recording.

The following checklist may help in the selection of a digital voice recorder:

- Is it intuitive and easy to use, or will it require a tutorial for each user?

- Is it easy to navigate to previously recorded files?

- Are the buttons and menu screen intuitive?

- Does it come with a strap or carrying case?

- Does it have at least 128MB in memory?

- Does it connect to the computer via a USB connection or cable? (Low-end digital recorders may not.)

- Is it compatible with my district's operating system?

- Does it download in a standard audio format, such as WAV or MP3?

- Is it compatible with Dragon Naturally Speaking™?

The Olympus line of digital voice recorders, which are compatible with Dragon Naturally Speaking and with Tool Factory Podcasting, are easy to use, with sound quality comparable to that of the iPod. An excellent Olympus model is the 300M (http://www.olympusamerica.com/cpg_section/product.asp?product= 1193), which retails for under $100. It runs for approximately 15 hours on a single

AAA battery, and the battery pack detaches to reveal a USB port for transferring files to a computer for editing. Unlike the iPod, an Olympus can be plugged into any computer's USB port, making it an excellent option for sharing among several teachers. Olympus saves its files in WMA (Windows Media Audio) format. Download the free Switch conversion software (http://www.nch.com.au/switch/) to convert the files to mp3 or WAV format, either of which can be used to import the file into Audacity for editing.

Cellular Phones with Built-in Voice Recorders

Cellular phones continue to add features without adding significantly to the purchase price. One of the newer features is a voice recorder, helping cellular phones position themselves as potential teaching and learning tools. Because cellular phones are expressly designed to filter out extraneous noise and deliver clear, crisp audio to the user, and because many students already own this technology, the use of cell phones as portable recorders is worth considering. The LG Chocolate phones marketed in 2006 and 2007 by Verizon, for example, generate WAV files of impressive quality.

To transfer files from the cell phone, a wireless Bluetooth connection, separate USB cable, or special data transfer subscription plan may be necessary. Educators considering bringing their cell phones to school may wish to consult with their cellular service provider or homeowner's insurance company regarding coverage if the phone is damaged or lost at school.

School policies regarding staff and student cell phone use must also be considered. Privacy factors—such as loaning a cell phone to students who can then access the teacher's list of recent and missed calls or address book—are also a consideration.

However, the use of cell phones for learning remains on the horizon as a promising consideration for the future.

▇ VOICE MAIL PODCASTS

Proving that there really is no barrier to podcasting at school is a series of Web sites that allow users to telephone a toll or toll-free number and leave voice mail messages that are converted into mp3 format and uploaded to the Web automatically. Gabcast.com and Gcast.com are among the companies that provide this service. Users create an account online and receive a PIN number. After dialing in and entering the PIN number, users leave a voice mail message (Chen 2007). These companies then convert the voice mail into an mp3 file and post it to the Web. They host up to around 200MB in files at no charge, with more hosting available for a fee. To maximize the amount of file space available, investigate the registration details to see if students can register their own accounts. Voice mail podcasts are particularly appealing for student projects that require podcasting from home, assuming that all students in the building have access to a telephone after school. If not, arrangements could be made with a local community center or library. Some voice mail podcasts have limited or no editing capabilities.

◼ CONCLUSION

With such a wide variety of software and hardware, there really are no barriers to making a podcast. The next chapters familiarize readers with the steps involved in making and publishing podcasts, from vocal warm-ups to recording tips to publication.

Chapter 4
Vocal Techniques and Strategies

■ INTRODUCTION

In its earliest days, podcasting was regarded primarily as a technological marvel. But step back for a moment: What else is a podcast? A *performance*. A *performing art*. Like other performing art forms, like choral music or drama, podcasting benefits from vocal warm-up techniques. Preparing the voice for performance strengthens vocal production and develops strong, flexible voices. Vocal warm-ups can relax the voice and vocal production muscles and also relax the students' minds, releasing anxiety and centering the mind. This can contribute to podcasts that sparkle with energy. This chapter explores relaxation techniques, vocal exercises that prepare the voice for performance, and tips for vocally rich podcasting performances.

■ RELAXATION TECHNIQUES

Stand in the hallway as classes pass. Close your eyes. What is that environment like? Loud lockers slamming? Students shouting at one another down the hall? The sharp clack of heels on linoleum floors? Teachers calling out, "Get to class!" The shrill of the late bell? This is the chaotic world that envelops many students as they arrive in classrooms.

Imagine yourself as a student, leaving that noisy din and stepping into your classroom as the teacher says, "OK, today we're going to make a podcast." Slam! Performance anxiety! The muscles tense. The throat struggles to gulp a new breath of air.

Relaxation techniques offer students the chance to center themselves physically and mentally while preparing the jaw, tongue, shoulders, and vocal cords for performance. They transition students from the turmoil outside the classroom into the secure, safe environment that has been created for them in the classroom. Try the following cycle of relaxation exercises:

- **Relax the jaw.** Ask students to pretend to yawn two or three times. Allow a gentle sound to escape during exhalation. The mouth opens wide; the area around the lips stretches, and the throat relaxes. Ancient yogis knew the value of this exercise: they incorporated it into their "Lion" yoga pose.

- **Massage the face, especially along the jawline.** This should be vigorous, with the metaphor of awakening the cells beneath the skin. Pay particular attention to the area where the upper and lower jaws come together in front of the ears.

- **Massage and "unfold" the ears.** Vigorously massage the earlobes and bend back the folds along the top of the earlobe. The earlobes should feel warm and tingly. Some practitioners believe that this loosens the back muscles as well.

- **Take a few deep breaths.** These should travel all the way down the torso into the belly. Breathe in through the nose and out through the mouth. As an optional addition, say, "Breathe out stress." A gentle sound during exhalation is appropriate. This exercise is wonderful to repeat just before pressing "Record" for a podcast, as it quickly lets out accumulated tension.

- **Loosen the shoulders.** Hunch up both shoulders, trying to get them as close to the ears as possible, creating a situation of maximum tension. Then breathe out, exhaling tension and releasing the shoulders to a low, relaxed position. Repeat two or three times. Roll the shoulders backwards, then forwards, then isolate one shoulder at a time.

These brief relaxation exercises calm the body and the mind.

■ VOCAL WARM-UPS

Now that the voice is relaxed, it can engage in exercises to make it more adept and skilled.

Tongue Twisters

The goal of tongue twisters is to strengthen *articulation*, that is, movement of the mouth and jaw to make clear, accurate sounds. This is essential for audio work, as podcast listeners cannot observe facial expressions or body language to assist in gaining meaning. Tongue twisters encourage *overarticulation*, that is, over-careful, exaggerated pronunciation and speech via careful manipulation of the lips, teeth, and tongue (Kelner and Flynn 2006).

One way to explain the concepts of articulation and overarticulation is to ask students to imagine that they are speaking to a colleague who has a hearing impairment and uses lip-reading to understand. Ask them to work in partners, with one student role-playing the person with the hearing impairment and the other trying to communicate. Switch roles. After the exercise, ask them to explain what they did with their lips, teeth, and tongue to make themselves understood—that is articulation.

Tongue twisters are an excellent way to practice articulation. The objective is clear speech, not speed. Rather than racing to the finish, students should concentrate on slow, clear delivery of the sounds. Repeat the tongue twisters again and again, slowly gaining speed without sacrificing articulation.

- Donny did dishes while Denny dabbled with darts.
- Ronnie wiped windows while Winnie wrote wish lists.
- Fred fried franks while Frank fried fritters.
- Polly practically put paprika in her peppermint.

For more tongue twisters, try the Tongue Twister database at http://www.geocities.com/athens/8136/tonguetwisters.html or engage students in writing their own using Leslie Opp-Beckman's tongue twister lesson at http://darkwing.uoregon.edu/~leslieob/twisters.html.

■ Vocal Variety

Vocal variety is a general term for manipulating the voice in different ways to change how it sounds (Fontichiaro 2007). By varying the speed, pitch, and volume of speech, the speaker can communicate a much richer message to the listener.

Pitch is the register of the voice, a range from low (think "Ol' Man River") to high (*Sesame Street's* Elmo). Wide ranges in pitch by novice podcasters can be difficult for listeners to understand. Artificial voices can also be difficult for students to reproduce accurately over a multiple-day recording session. In addition, student performers can create vocal strain if they attempt pitches outside their vocal range. For most informational podcasting projects, encourage the use of the students' relaxed, natural voices.

However, pitch is a fundamental tool for establishing character in a drama podcast such as a radio play. High-pitched voices are often considered to be child-like, happy, or anxious, while low-pitched voices can be perceived as adult, all-knowing, somber, or sad. To maximize comprehension when adopting a character voice, students should slow down their speaking. To assist students in slowing down their speech, a useful exercise is to ask them to rehearse the script once through as if in slow motion. This helps relax the muscles, quell nerves, and slow down the speech pattern.

Speed is the rapidity or slowness of a person's speech. Especially for nervous podcasters delivering informational text, there is often a tendency to rush, creating an oral delivery that sounds nervous or anxious. To assist students in slowing down, consider highlighting end punctuation in the script using a highlighter or red pen. These marks will serve as visual reminders to pause between sentences, phrases, or clauses. Encourage students to take a quiet breath (not a loud exhalation that will be picked up by the microphone) at the end of each sentence or phrase.

Volume is the loudness or softness of the voice. Many young podcasters are hesitant to speak loudly and clearly, especially when surrounded by classmates. Encourage students to speak confidently and authoritatively, assuming the role of an expert. Volume can be controlled by the human voice, by adjusting the volume using software, or by changing the distance between the mouth and the microphone.

Energy or *tone* is affiliated with emotion and emphasis. It's the extra "oomph" that carries our meaning into our voice. Emotions like happiness, sadness, loneliness, and fear can be expressed through the voice.

Energy can be one of the greatest challenges, especially for adolescent podcasters. Many students have a tendency to begin a sentence with high energy, but by the end of the sentence, their energy has dipped and the last few words of the sentence are mumbled. Encourage them to sustain energy throughout the entire sentence. Students with a tendency to drop off the ends of sentences can draw a rising arrow over the last few words as a reminder to continue to push the sound energy through right up until the end of the sentence.

The type of end punctuation—a period, exclamation point, or question mark—is also a visual clue to help students build up energy at the appropriate point of a sentence. Another energy tool that aids in comprehension is asking students to go through their scripts and circle or highlight the key words. This also serves as a visual reminder during the recording process to give a word an extra boost of energy and attention. This tool is particularly useful when recording persuasive texts such as advertisements.

■ CONCLUSION

The vocal exercises and strategies discussed in this chapter can assist students in creating podcasts that are performances, not just recordings. They add sparkle, animation, and personality to school podcasts.

Chapter 5
Recording a Simple Podcast

◼ INTRODUCTION

This chapter explores the basic steps and strategies for recording a simple podcast on a desktop or laptop computer. With the click of a few buttons, the user is well on the way to becoming a successful podcaster. This chapter focuses specifically on Audacity software, because it is open-source software available without charge, can be downloaded on both Macintosh and Windows platforms (going as far back as Windows 98 and the Mac 0S9 operating systems), can quickly be scaled throughout a building at no cost, and is the most commonly referenced podcasting software in educational technology literature.

◼ DOWNLOADING THE SOFTWARE

Audacity is a free download from http://audacity.sourceforge.net. Because it is open-source software, updated versions are frequently available. If given the option between a stable version of Audacity, which has already been tested and shown to be relatively free of programming bugs, and a beta version, which might offer more features but be less stable, it is recommended that schools download the stable version.

Audacity lets the user import, record, and mix sounds. However, exporting the finished product into mp3 format requires the free LAME converter. Licensing issues preclude LAME's converter from being incorporated into Audacity, so follow the online instructions and download LAME. Extract the compressed LAME file and install it in an out-of-the-way place on the hard drive. The first time you ask Audacity to export the file to mp3 (FILE > EXPORT AS MP3), Audacity will ask you to locate the LAME converter. Once you have navigated to the LAME file and selected it, Audacity remembers the location and never asks for this step again.

To make podcasting as easy as possible for students, locate the LAME converter for Audacity before students use Audacity for the first time.

■HELPING AUDACITY RUN EFFICIENTLY

On computers that are less than three years old, Audacity runs without a hitch. However, older computers with slower processors may have greater difficulty processing sound input. This can cause delays or hang-ups while recording. To maximize the efficiency of Audacity in processing and editing sound, try these tips, recommended by the Audacity wiki (http://audacityteam.org/wiki):

1. **Close all other programs except Audacity while recording.**

2. **Schedule automatic software or antivirus updates so they will not occur during your recording times.**

3. **Reduce the bit depth.** *Bit depth* is the amount of data processed for each piece of sound information, and it can consume the processor speed of an older computer. Reducing the bit depth while recording new content or importing existing content can reduce the stress on the computer's processor. Go to FILE > PREFERENCES > QUALITY and change Default Sample Format from 32 bit (the default setting) to 16 bit.

4. **Record in mono.** For voice recordings, you can save file size and processing speed if you record in mono, not stereo. (Recording in mono also streamlines the look of your project on the screen.) However, if you plan to record multiple voices or instruments, you may wish to switch back to stereo recording mode. To set Audacity to record in mono format, go to FILE > PREFERENCES > AUDIO I/O. For "Channels," select "1 (Mono)."

5. **Turn off the waveform display while recording**. By its default setting, Audacity creates and displays *waveforms* (the graphical representation of sound waves) when recording. While it is useful to see these waves during the editing process, the constant redrawing of the waveforms can consume valuable processor energy. Go to FILE > PREFERENCES and uncheck the "Auto-scroll while playing" option.

6. **Turn off the meter toolbar while recording**. The meter toolbar displays the strength of the incoming audio signal and is not necessary for basic podcasting. In fact, when working with easily distracted students, such as those with attention deficit disorder (ADD), it may be useful to disable the meter toolbar regardless of the age or processing speed of the computer being used. Go to FILE > PREFERENCES and uncheck "Enable Meter Toolbar."

7. **Disable the screensaver if making a long recording.** Screensavers can sometimes "freeze" an Audacity project when they activate. To turn off a screensaver in Windows XP, go to START > CONTROL PANEL > DISPLAY > SCREENSAVER tab. From the pull-down menu under "Screen Saver," select "None." Click OK.

If these simple solutions are not effective, consult the extensive list at http://audacityteam.org/wiki/index.php?title=Managing_Computer_Resources_ and_Drivers.

◼ SETTING UP FOR A PODCAST

Once students have prepared the necessary script or text (see Chapters 8 to 14), they are ready to podcast.

Scripts should be printed in a large font (such as 18 point) and double-spaced for ease of reading. Fonts such as Times New Roman and Comic Sans are particularly easy to read.

Encourage students to participate in a few vocal warm-ups or tongue twisters until their voices are limber, and have them mark their scripts with reminders for sustained sounds, key words to highlight, end punctuation, and pauses. See Chapter 4 for more details.

Next, set up the microphone(s). Be sure the microphone is turned on (if there is an on/off switch) and that the volume has been turned up all the way. Headsets should be adjusted so that the microphone portion is approximately one to two inches from the student's mouth, and the cords should be long enough so that students have some freedom of movement. This is particularly important for elementary students, who tend to be more physically active and animated during the podcasting process. Use sanitizing phone wipes or household disinfecting wipes to clean headsets between use. If multiple students will be recording at a single computer station, use Y adapters, as discussed in Chapter 3, to connect multiple headsets into a single set of microphone and headphone jacks.

Arrange the students' chairs so they can easily see the screen and the sound waves that will appear there during the recording process. Some students are more comfortable standing while they podcast, and because this facilitates better breath control, it is an acceptable option. Appoint one student to operate the mouse and control the recording to avoid confusion or squabbling over this task.

Set all scripts down on the table. The keyboard is not needed during recording, so it can be moved out of the way if necessary, or the script may be placed on top of it. Handheld scripts can create unintended windlike sounds during recording.

Now encourage students to take a few deep breaths in through the nose and out through the mouth. The first step is for them to create and listen to a sample recording.

■ USING AUDACITY TO RECORD

To make a basic recording, students need to understand the basic "buttons" on the top toolbar. These are intuitively designed to resemble boom box or cassette recorder buttons. From left to right, the buttons represent SKIP TO START (returns the cursor to the start of the podcast), PLAY (starts playing back the podcast beginning at the point where the cursor is), RECORD, PAUSE, STOP, and SKIP TO THE END of the podcast. To see a button's purpose, hover the mouse over it.

Once students are familiar with the basic operating buttons, they can make a sample recording to examine the sound levels. Begin by clicking on the red RECORD button. Up at the top, the sound input and output meters will show the various input and output levels (unless these were turned off to maximize processing speed), but these can be ignored. As the podcaster speaks, a sound track with waveforms appears in the middle of the screen. The louder the sound input into the computer, the larger the waveforms. Press the brown STOP button when finished.

Checking Sound Levels

Now check the sound levels. Click the first round button on the toolbar. This is the SKIP TO START button and will return the cursor to the start of the recording. Push PLAY to review what has been heard. Listen and watch the waveforms. As shown on page 38, the optimal waveform does not fill the entire track, nor does it make tiny waves. If the waveform exceeds the track, stop recording by pushing the brown square STOP button. Click the "X" in the far left corner of the track to delete it. Move the microphone farther away from the person speaking and try again. If the waveform is weak, press STOP, delete the track, and move the microphone closer to the person speaking or encourage the speaker to speak louder. If the waveform appears as a horizontal line, no sound input has been received. Check to make sure that the microphone or headset has been plugged in completely and correctly. Keep in mind that Audacity cannot process both a USB and a $\frac{1}{8}$-inch jack microphone simultaneously.

Additional buttons that are useful for recording are PAUSE and SKIP TO THE END. Use PAUSE when the podcast is interrupted or when playing back. Use SKIP TO THE END when you wish to continue adding to an existing recording.

Making a Podcast with Audacity

1. Prepare for the recording session. Plug in the microphone. If it has an on/off switch, turn it on. If there is a volume control, turn it all the way up. Turn on the computer and open the Audacity software. Set scripts down on the table to avoid rustling noises during the recording session. Take a deep breath and get ready to record.

2. Record. When ready, click on the red "RECORD" button on the top menu and begin to speak. Notice the blue sound wave pattern appearing midway down the screen. If it is a flat line, it is not picking up any sound. When it is picking up sound, blue sound waves will appear. Try to speak loudly enough (or put the microphone closer to your mouth) so that the blue waves fill up about half of the recording bar. The first time you use Audacity, you may wish to record just the opening words of your project to test the sound levels. Click the STOP button on the top menu when you have finished recording.

3. Review what has been recorded. Click the REWIND button (two triangles pointing left). If the recording sounds good, continue with the next step. If not, go to FILE > NEW and start over again.

4. Edit out "blank air" moments, where the blue sound wave appears horizontal. Highlight the part you want to delete. Then click EDIT > CUT.

5. Add music or record a sound effects track. Creativecommons.org has a searchable list of music that can be downloaded and used wihtout charge for educational or podcasting projects. To add downloaded music, go to PROJECT > IMPORT AUDIO and navigate to the music file. Make creative sound effects from scraps of wood, musical instruments, noisemakers, or toys. Record sound effects on a separate track from the spoken word track to facilitate editing. To do this, set Audacity to play back the first track when adding a second. Go to FILE > PREFERENCES > AUDIO I/O , check "Play other tracks while recording," and click OK. After the speaking parts are recorded, click the REWIND button (two left-pointing triangles). Then push RECORD. A new track will appear under the speech track. The recorded text will be heard so that the sound effects can be placed in precisely the right spot. If corrections need to be made, just record the affected track rather than starting from scratch.

6. Save project and export as an mp3 file. Audacity saves its files in its own unique file format. Use FILE > SAVE PROJECT to save large projects periodically. To be used for burning a CD, importing to iTunes, e-mailing, or posting online, the file must then be exported into mp3 format. Go to FILE > EXPORT AS MP3 and decide where to save it and what file name to give it. Click SAVE. The first time an mp3 is made, Audacity will prompt the user to identify where the LAME converter is stored. See the downloading instructions at http://audacity.sourceforge.net for details.

7. Add metadata to the file. Metadata is a collection of words that describe the audio file. Metadata is useful when your file is imported into iTunes; it will be the information that appears about your file (the document name assigned in Step 6 will not appear). A dialog box will pop up asking for some information. For TITLE, give the name of the student's work (i.e., "Pioneer radio play"). For ARTIST, give just a first name, class ("third grade"), or even a student number. Don't use specific names that you don't want strangers to have access to, as this information will travel with the mp3 file wherever it goes. For ALBUM, type the name of the overall class project, like "Radio2008." (Keep this to one easily spelled word to minimize student error.) Select "Spoken Word" for the genre. Click OK to finish.

Uploading to an iPod *or* Burning a CD

1. Add the mp3 file to iTunes. Open iTunes. Go to FILE > IMPORT... to add the file to iTunes. Now build a playlist. A playlist is like a documents folder: it holds virtual copies of your audio recordings; however, a single audio file can be "stored" in multiple playlists. So Jacquie's radio play can be filed in the Radio Plays playlist *and* in the Jacquie2008 playlist for easy retrieval. Go to FILE > NEW PLAYLIST. Now click and drag your mp3 files into the proper playlist. (The mp3 files will also still appear on the main iTunes Library screen.)

2. Burn a CD. Double-click on the playlist you want. Insert a blank CD. Click the Burn CD button in the top right corner of iTunes.

3. Transfer files to an iPod. Connect the iPod to the computer. When the iPod icon appears in the left column, drag the playlist onto the iPod icon.

Publishing to the Web

Uploading files to the Web requires online storage space. Many school districts have Web sites that allow teachers to upload any kind of file to a teacher's Web site. If not, discuss other online storage options with the system administrator. One free option is Switchpod (http://www.switchpod.com). Once the audio file is uploaded, place a link to it on a blog or the Web site. Technically, a podcast is like a magazine subscription: subscribers find the podcast series to which they wish to subscribe, and subsquent podcasts added to the series are downloaded automatically by the user's software. This requires setting up an RSS feed using a tool such as Feedburner (http://www.feedburner.com). To protect students' privacy, be cautious about allowing them to record personal information on a podcast.

These instructions were written for Audacity for Windows XP and iTunes 7.0.2 for Windows. Instructions for other operating systems are similar.

Top Row: Mixer Toolbar (ignore for most basic podcasts)

Bottom Row, L to R: Cut, Copy, Paste, Trim Outside Selection, Silence, Insert Silence, Undo, Redo, Zoom In, Zoom Out, Fit Selection in Window, Fit Project in Window

Timeline

A horizontal line indicates that the computer is not receiving any sound. Check the microphone connections.

Sound waves that consistently fill the entire track indicate that the sound input is too loud. Move the microphone further away or move the "…+" slider to the left.

These waveforms are just right.

Each of the shaded bars above is a separate track. To hear one track while recording the next one, go to FILE > PREFERENCES > AUDIO I/O and check the box marked "Play other tracks while recording new one."

Cursor Location (in minutes and seconds)

Top row: Selection Tool (click it, then highlight waveforms for editing), Envelope Tool (to adjust volume over time), Draw Tool

Recording buttons (L to R): Skip to Beginning, Play, Record, Pause, Stop, Skip to End)

Input and Output Meters (ignore for most basic podcasts; can be turned off)

This row: Zoom tool, Time Shift Tool (to move the location of one track), Multi-Tool Mode

Use this slider to adjust the volume of an individual track.

Click on the "X" to delete a track. Click the down arrow to give the track a name.

Screenshot of Audacity for Windows XP. The visual appearance of Audacity is slightly different for other operating systems.

Recording the Spoken Podcast

Once levels have been tested, students are ready to record their voices. Go to FILE > NEW (CTRL+N) to open a new document. Press RECORD to begin and STOP to end. Follow the instructions on page 37. Using the SELECTION tool, highlight and cut out any mistakes using EDIT>CUT (CTRL+X).

Adding Sound Effects or Music

Audacity was designed to record musical ensembles, with each instrument receiving its own track. Tracks are not only the songs found on a CD but also the individual recording lines found in audio editing software. The screenshot on page 38 shows a project with three tracks, noted by three shaded bars.

Similarly, when sound effects or music are added to a project, they will receive their own track. First, download the desired audio to the desktop or hard drive. An excellent source for podcast-friendly sound effects is A1 Free Sound Effects (http://www.a1freesoundeffects.com/radio.html). A great selection of music and loops can be found at Magnatune (http://www.magnatune.com). Follow the onscreen instructions for download.

Next, select PROJECT > IMPORT AUDIO from the top menu bar. Navigate to the downloaded audio file. Audacity will automatically create a new track and import the audio. To align the music with a specific place in the text, click on the SHIFT tool (double-headed arrow in top right corner), then click and drag the music's waveforms to the desired location.

Use the same technique to add audio files downloaded from a portable recording device.

Editing Audio

Often when adding a musical background to a podcast, there will be extra music at the end. Use the SELECTION tool to highlight and cut (EDIT > CUT or CTRL+X) the unwanted music, leaving a few extra seconds of music at the end. Highlight those few seconds using the SELECTION tool, then go to EFFECT > FADE OUT for a professional ending. Alternatively, customize the fadeout by selecting the ENVELOPE tool. Click on the track to adjust the fade out.

Sometimes when recording multiple tracks, one track may appear significantly louder or softer than another. For example, background music is desired, but it should fade into the background. In this case, use the slider on the far left of the track, as shown on page 38, to adjust the volume of a single track.

To amplify just one portion of a track, highlight it with the SELECTION tool, then select EFFECT > AMPLIFY. Adjust the level of amplification to find a palatable balance between increased sound and a hissing sound. The EFFECT menu has many other options for changing the quality of sound of selected waveforms.

■ SAVING A PROJECT

When users select FILE > SAVE PROJECT, the project will be saved as a data file with .aup as the file extension. In addition, a folder of data will be saved with the same file name. Saving the project is a different step from exporting to mp3. Save projects only if students are creating a project that will extend over more than one class session. If students are creating a project in a single sitting, it may not be necessary to save the project before exporting it into mp3 format.

■ EXPORTING THE PODCAST

Files with the .aup extension are fully editable. Each track can be edited, deleted, or changed. However, .aup files are not Web friendly, as they can only be played if the listener has Audacity installed on his or her computer. To make the podcast accessible to all listeners, it should be converted into the mp3 file format, a process known as *exporting*. Exporting does not replace the original Audacity file; rather, it makes an additional file in mp3 format.

When editing is complete, select FILE > EXPORT AS MP3. Choose a one-word name for the podcast with no spaces or capital letters in the name and select a location to save the file. Click SAVE. (See the notes earlier in this chapter for locating the LAME converter the first time Audacity attempts an export to mp3.)

A new window will pop up. This window asks for information about the podcast that will be embedded into the final mp3 file. This information is referred to as *metadata*. The information provided in this window will appear when the file is imported into iTunes or played with a desktop music player, so it should be chosen carefully. For the metadata, capital letters and spaces are acceptable. The following information is requested:

- **Format.** Leave this set at the "more flexible" default.

- **Title.** This is the name of the podcast, such as "Siberian Monkey" or "September 25 Show."

- **Album.** If the podcast is part of the class project, such as "Animal Reports," use the project name for the album. If it is a radio broadcast, consider giving it the title of the show, for example, "Kennedy School Live," using the date of the episode as the title.

- **Track number and year.** These are optional. Assigning a track number can help if a collection of files will be turned into a CD.

- **Genre.** This is a pull-down menu. "Speech" is the best match. A shortcut for Windows XP is to click on the down arrow, then hit the Page Down button seven times until "Speech" appears as an option.

- **Comments.** This can be left blank.

After inputting the metadata, click "OK." The file will be exported. For publishing options for the completed mp3 files, see Chapter 6.

Exporting a file to mp3 significantly reduces the overall size of the file. Smaller files function more efficiently online. However, the process of shrinking the file means the individual tracks will no longer be editable in the mp3 format, though the Audacity version will still be fully editable. (Think of a sandwich. When first made, the layers can still be pried apart. But if it has been smushed, the layers can no longer be separated.)

■ CONCLUSION

Recording a podcast is a simple process. With the file recorded, it is ready for sharing, the topic of the next chapter.

Chapter 6
Publishing and Distributing Podcasts

■ INTRODUCTION

This chapter explores various techniques for publishing and distributing podcasts. *Distribution* refers to the sharing of a podcast with others. A single podcast can be shared almost instantly with a limitless number of listeners. Traditionally, podcasts have been posted online and "subscribed to" by listeners who use an RSS feed and a podcast aggregating service such as iTunes or iPodder that automatically delivers new episodes when they are created. However, there are many other options for distributing podcasts that are useful to the K–12 educator. These include leaving the file on the computer on which it was created, e-mailing the file, burning the file to an audio CD, uploading the file and creating a link to a Web page or blog, and creating an RSS feed, as mentioned earlier. These methods are nonexclusive: A single file can be shared in any or all of these ways. This flexibility helps educators reach the proper audience for each podcast.

■ OPTION ONE: CREATE A LISTENING KIOSK

This option is particularly appealing for elementary or self-contained classrooms. In these classrooms, there is often flexible time built into the schedule for "centers," that is, small learning stations scattered about the room among which students rotate. In this case, the easiest way for students to hear a podcast is simply to walk up to the computer and listen to the podcast, much as convention attendees might walk up to an informational kiosk. Teacher-created podcasts work quite well for this arrangement, but they can be used for student podcasts as well.

The fastest way to set up a kiosk is to create a shortcut to the mp3 file on the computer's desktop. Leave a brief set of instructions next to the computer for older students or lead a brief demonstration for younger students. Be sure young students know how to work the computer's audio listening software to pause, rewind, or play the selection again.

Following are some projects that work well with kiosk-based podcasts:

- **Spelling or other oral test makeups.** An elementary teacher realizes that two students are absent. Rather than allot future time for a makeup test, she records herself orally administering the test to the rest of the class. When the absent students return, they visit the kiosk and play back the recording.

- **Instructions for a game or activity.** Many elementary curriculum kits include games or activities that can be used for enrichment. Young children who are not yet fluent readers may struggle to read the instructions independently and call on their teacher to read them to them. Instead, the instructor can record the instructions and invite the students to listen the instructions, building independence and reserving teacher time for other concerns.

- **Parent-teacher conferences.** Engage waiting parents by rolling a computer outside the classroom. Post a simple set of instructions so they can listen to their children's work.

- **Sponge activities.** A "sponge activity" is designed to keep K–12 students occupied when they first arrive in a classroom and the instructor is preoccupied with attendance or other housekeeping activities. The teacher can record some oral dictation in advance and push "play" as students enter the classroom. Recorded sponge activities can help students review basic skills or recall-level facts in preparation for a deeper interaction of content with teachers later in the lesson. A benefit is that the students must enter the room quietly in order to hear the recorded content! Try one of these sponge activities:

  - **Chemistry.** The instructor reads off a list of elements; the students write the abbreviations (or vice versa). The instructor can also call out a compound, such as "sodium chloride," and students must write down the formula (or vice versa).

  - **Social studies.** The teacher records the names of states. When the file is played back, the students write the capitals (or vice versa). Or the teacher records the names of presidents and the students write the name of the previous or next president or the years in office.

  - **Language arts.** The teacher reads a sentence; the students identify and write the subject, verb, prepositional phrase, or other part of speech. With older students, the teacher could record metaphors or similes embedded in the previous night's homework assignment and ask students to define what they mean. For students studying for the SAT, consider a recording that states, defines, uses in a sentence, and spells advanced vocabulary words.

  - **Physical education.** The teacher records a calisthenics or warm-up drill or a yoga sun salute.

  - **Music.** Vocal warm-ups are recorded, with pauses after each scale so that students can sing it back. For secondary music appreciation students, the teacher records himself or herself playing an excerpt from a given musical era, and students are asked to identify the period and explain their answers.

- **Number/letter recognition.** Kindergarteners and first graders need practice matching written numbers and letters with their oral equivalents. Create Bingo cards for each student. In the recording, the teacher randomly calls out letters or numbers and asks students to mark their cards. Vary the recording and cards to ensure that students are not memorizing patterns.

- **Library/media center.** The librarian, staff members, or students record brief booktalks about favorite books. Students can visit the booktalk kiosk to find recommendations.

■ OPTION TWO: E-MAIL THE FILE

E-mailing is a great way to get a podcast heard quickly, as most people check their e-mail many times a day. Simply append the mp3 file to an e-mail like any other attachment. If the podcasts are smaller than 2MB, the file can be e-mailed to others. Most e-mail programs will accept a file of up to this size without rejecting it. Files larger than 2MB may be rejected by the recipient's system. Be sure to check with your district technology office before sending podcasts via e-mail to find out about the maximum file size an individual can send or receive.

Following are some cases in which sending a podcast via e-mail might be effective:

- **Recording quick samples of student reading fluency or speech patterns for a district expert.** This can help when a classroom teacher seeks outside expertise in evaluating the skill levels of a student. A reading specialist or speech therapist housed at the central office can quickly review the file and send feedback within hours, whereas burning and sending a CD or scheduling a face-to-face appointment might take much longer.

- **Sharing great work with parents or administrators.** From time to time, podcasting brings out something remarkably wonderful in an otherwise lackluster student. Or a student struggling with a certain subject area suddenly reveals a moment of clarity while recording a podcast, and the educator knows the delight and relief this will bring to a parent. The podcast might not be suited to public posting, so sharing it via e-mail is more appropriate.

There is one caveat to e-mailing: District e-mail may be considered public information, to which others may request access. Check with your district's technology services department.

■ OPTION THREE: BURN A CD

Especially if there are parental or administrative concerns about posting student work online, a CD compilation of student podcasts is a viable alternative. CDs are quite inexpensive. A pack of 50 can cost about $10, or 20 cents a disk. Busy parents who might not have time to sit at a kiosk or even to download a podcast at home can pop the CD into their car stereo and listen with their children while running errands.

There are two ways to burn a CD. One is merely to create a data disc using the CD authoring (burning) software that comes standard with many computers, copying the mp3 files onto a CD. This creates an mp3 CD. Mp3 CDs can be played by many newer CD players and DVD players, but they do not work on older, legacy CD players (look for the word "mp3" in the specifications for your player). A more universal option is to use audio software that creates *audio* CDs, converting the mp3 files into a format that can be played on all CD players. This is a more practical option.

While many audio listening programs, including Windows Media Player, which ships as part of the standard Windows operating system, give users the option to burn an audio CD, Apple's iTunes has an elegant, simple interface and cross-platform functionality. iTunes is available as a free download from http://www.apple.com/itunes.

To begin, add the mp3 files to the iTunes library. This creates a link between the stored mp3 file and the iTunes interface. This can be done by selecting FILE > IMPORT or FILE > ADD FILE TO LIBRARY and navigating to the current location of the file. Repeat this process for each file. The files now appear in the main iTunes Music Library window, a master listing of all audio files maintained by iTunes. (To navigate back to the Music Library at any time, select "Music" under the "Library" heading in the left navigation column.)

In Chapter 5, as files were exported into mp3 format, Audacity asked for a Title, Artist, Album, and Genre to be assigned. Notice how iTunes displays this information for each recording, *not* the file name, making it much easier to navigate and select files. Clicking the words "Name," "Artist," "Album," or "Genre" at the top of the iTunes library screen lets one sort the order in which the items display.

The next step is to create a playlist. iTunes must have items organized in a playlist before it will burn the disc. Playlists allow the user to select and group together certain items from the master Music Library. To create a playlist, select FILE > NEW PLAYLIST (or CTRL+N on a PC) and give the playlist a descriptive name like "Amazing Animals" or "Civil War." The playlist will show up in the left navigation column under the "Playlists" heading. Click on the name of a podcast and drag the file into the playlist. The name of the file will still remain on the master Library page, but it will also show up when the playlist name is clicked on. Repeat until all desired files are in the playlist.

Now click on the playlist name, and the list of files affiliated with that playlist will show up in the main window. Check the list of files to make sure none are missing, then click the "Burn Disc" button at the bottom of the screen. Follow the onscreen instructions, and a few moments later, the CD is complete. Burning multiple copies through iTunes can be somewhat time consuming. It is generally faster to create subsequent copies of the audio CD by using duplication software.

One of the reasons why iTunes is great for managing student podcast files is that a single mp3 file can be linked to dozens of playlists. This means that a podcast called "Sophia's Animal Report" could be placed both in the Animal Reports Playlist and in the Sophia Playlist. At the end of the Animal Reports unit, the teacher or school library media specialist could burn a CD from the Animal Reports Playlist for checkout in the library, and at the end of the year, the Sophia Playlist could be burned to a CD and placed in her permanent record. In addition, iTunes makes it easy to sort by album (Animal Reports) or artist (Sophia). This portfolio approach is useful to track reading fluency or writing skill over time.

Before the CD is "released," it is fun to ask kids to pitch in. They can design their own CD label or album art, using markers or colored pencils or an online template, such as those available from the Avery Dennison label company (http://www.avery.com). Labels can also be preprinted by the teacher with the album name, with students adding their own original art in the margins.

In the music industry, a CD release is launched with fanfare, including promotional posters and a CD release party. Enlist students and parents to organize a CD release party and publicize it with student-made posters and invitations to school administrators, board members, and community leaders. Toss in a few refreshments and a few congratulatory speeches, and the CD is well on its way to going platinum.

After the release, donate a copy to the school library for checkout. Students, especially those in elementary and middle school, feel validated as "real" content creators when their work is included in the media center collection.

■ OPTION FOUR: UPLOAD THE FILE AND LINK IT TO A WEB PAGE

The next few options discussed are more traditional podcasting routes. In general, there are two things required to post a podcast online. First, it requires server space, which is essentially a place to store the file. Second, it requires a Web page. Listeners will be directed to the Web page and click on a link to hear the podcast.

Identify Server Space

Most educational podcasts will be uploaded to the Web and shared with people outside the school community. *Uploading* means putting a copy of the podcast file online, then linking to it from a Web site or blog. A server is a huge "hard drive" that stores online files and makes them accessible to listeners via the Web. "Server space" is the amount of storage space allocated to you on a server, measured in megabytes, gigabytes, or terabytes.

To best determine the type of server space most appropriate for you, it is important to begin by understanding file size. Most podcasts will average 3 to 10 megabytes (MB). By comparison, a photo taken with a 4-megapixel camera will average 1.5MB. A gigabyte (GB) is equivalent to 1,000 megabytes, and a terabyte is equivalent to 1,000 gigabytes.

Therefore, if the school district provides 10MB of server space per user, which was generous in the early days of Web design, it will be inadequate for uploading podcasts. If you plan to make 100 or more podcasts throughout the course of a year, a minimum of a gigabyte of space is recommended. It is possible to podcast with less space, but that will require taking older podcasts off the server, providing little opportunity for listeners to see the growth of the students over the course of an academic year.

Another important consideration is protecting students' rights as copyright holders for their materials. Students, even as minors, own the copyright to any work that they make. Educators are trustees of their intellectual property rights. Important questions to ask are, "Who should have control over my students' intellectual assets?" and, "Who has the power to remove a podcast?" Free Web hosting software might be least expensive, but ultimately, the host controls access to your students' work. Answering these questions often leads to the conclusion that buying server space is the best choice, because district employees control file access and have a clearly defined plan for backing up files.

To find the best server space option for you, consider each of these provider options: the school district's existing server space, a free podcast-hosting provider, or purchased server space. Each of these offers advantages and disadvantages.

▶ District-Provided Web Space

Your district's technology services department can help determine whether district Web space is available for uploading podcasts. If servers have been upgraded recently, this may be possible. In addition, you may find a kindred spirit in the technology office, someone interested in exploring this technology. He or she may be eager to share experiences.

However, the district may not be able to provide server space. Many school districts are on a fixed cycle for technology upgrades. When the last technology upgrade occurred, the concept of posting audio or video online might not have even been envisioned. At the time of the last upgrade, many of the Internet-connected households in the district might have been operating on dial-up modems, making these large files almost impossible to view at home. At the time, the question, "Why post something online that hardly anyone can access outside of school?" was a legitimate one.

If the district has a content management system (CMS), a series of templates that guides the overall "look" of content across classrooms and schools in the district, it may also be limited in the types of files that can be uploaded.

If your district cannot host mp3 files, consider purchasing outside server space (see "Buying Server Space," page 49) as a temporary solution, until the next technology upgrade.

▶ Free Podcasting Hosting Sites

Many sites will provide about 200 MB of file space at no charge, which is equivalent to approximately 50 small podcasts, or about one small podcast a week for a single school year. Usually, for a small fee, additional file storage space can be purchased. To use one of these sites, visit and create a new account. Because of your role as steward of your students' intellectual property rights, be sure to read all of the rules and regulations before agreeing to the account. Then follow the online instructions for uploading files. Be sure to write down the URL (the Web address beginning with http://www) when the file is uploaded, as you will need it to create the link from your Web page or blog. Popular free podcast hosting sites include

Switchpod (http://www.switchpod.com),

Podbean (http://www.podebean.com),

PodOmatic (http://www.podomatic.org), and

Google Pages (http://pages.google.com)

One other important fact about these free hosting sites is that they provide free hosting to *anyone*. Some of the content hosted by a free site may not be appropriate for students to encounter. Be sure to explore each company's home page to be sure that you are comfortable with the featured content. If you send a link to a podcast hosted by a free site, some listeners might "peel back" the URL (e.g., if you send them http://www.podbean.com/myschool/mygreatpodcast.mp3, they might remove the end of the URL and visit http:/www.podbean.com). Be sure you are comfortable with what users might find if this happens.

▶ Buying Server Space

In recent years, competition in the Web hosting business has led to terrific bargains for those wishing to buy Web space. There are two options for purchasing.: First is to buy a dedicated server, meaning a huge hard drive stored somewhere in the world where every bit of content is yours. This is more than most schools will need. The second option is to buy space on a server, knowing that other users have access to other parts of the server, but not your files. This option is both affordable and provides ample storage space. $100 generally buys these features:

- Registration of the domain name (e.g., mygreatschool.com)

- One year of hosting service

- 24-7 tech support, including Web-based chat, phone support, and support via e-mail

- Instructions for how to upload your files using a Web-based uploading system or file transfer protocol (FTP)

- At least a terabyte of space

- Additional tools and features that may be useful, such as the ability to host a blog on the site, Web site templates, or photo management software

- Additional tools and features that may not be relevant to schools, such as the ability to host an online store

Generally, there is a minimal discount given for purchasing more than one year's worth of hosting at a time. Given that many districts will upgrade their in-district hosting space in the next few years as a result of the next planned technology grade, consider buying just one year's worth of hosting at a time. Most Web providers send automatic e-mail reminders when the account is up for renewal. Some even send early renewal incentives. To avoid surprises, however, mark the renewal date in your calendar.

Many companies sell Web hosting. Check the ads at the back of a computer magazine for ideas or ask friends for recommendations. Two of the more established companies used by educators are Globat (http://www.globat.com) and GoDaddy (http://www.godaddy.com). Both offer competitive pricing and features. One particularly nice feature of Globat is that it offers a user-friendly file management system via the Web, which lets the site administrator assign unique passwords to different folders and restrict folder access to particular users. This means that if an entire building is sharing one Web domain, Mrs. Jones would have access only to her online folder within the site, and Mr. Smith would have access only to his. Meanwhile, the designated site administrator would be able to access all files.

Print out the e-mail that is sent after the Web site registration is complete and store it in a safe place. It will contain important information about login and passwords, renewal information, tech support numbers, and getting started with the Web site.

▶ *File Management*

File management refers to the process of organizing documents and folders to facilitate easy retrieval at a later date. Whenever a user saves a file into the "Taxes" folder of his or her My Documents, he or she is practicing file management. Whenever he or she just saves directly into My Documents, resulting in a long list of unsorted documents, there is no file management. Just as with physical documents, digital documents can be sorted into folders by topic or category. The same is true with documents, including podcasts, uploaded to a server.

If you upload documents via a CMS, file management will likely be done automatically, without your knowledge. But if you are using free hosting space or purchasing server space from a Web hosting provider, a basic understanding of file management will make podcast storage much more efficient.

Like its desktop counterpart, server storage space can be divided into hierarchical folders. With a Web provider like Globat, the main folder may be automatically created and named *httpdocs,* and the folder name should not be changed if it is present. "Httpdocs" is shorthand for "hypertext transfer protocol documents." All files should be saved inside the httpdocs folder. If there is no "httpdocs" folder, then it is safe to assume that files can be stored anywhere.

If you plan on making dozens, perhaps hundreds, of podcasts over the course of the year, it is useful to sort projects into folders. To do this, use your Web provider's Web-based file management system or, if none is provided, open Internet Explorer for PC and type the FTP address given you by your Web host. Mac users may wish to purchase an inexpensive FTP software called Transmit, for approximately $30, available for download at http://www.panic.com/transmit.

If using FTP, type the login and password when requested. To create a new folder, go to FILE > NEW FOLDER. Type the name of the folder, using lowercase letters only, no apostrophes or commas, and no spaces. (Underline marks and hyphens work fine.) To add files to that folder, double-click on it to open it, then copy and paste the podcast files into it.

To create a link to the podcast you've just uploaded, you will need to know that podcast's unique URL. Imagine that you own a domain name called mygreatschooltestsite.org. Inside your httpdocs folder (or at the top level if there is no httpdocs folder) is a subfolder called beckyspodcasts (remember, no capital letters, apostrophes, or spaces between words. Inside the beckyspodcasts folder, there is a file called flowerpoem.mp3. The resulting URL would be http://www.mygreatschooltestsite.org/beckyspodcasts/flowerpoem.mp3.

Each part of the address must be recorded perfectly in order for the link to work.

▶ Adding the Link to the Web Page

Once the file is uploaded, log into the Web site. In addition to creating a link to the podcast, it is recommended that you create a brief summary of the podcast. Just as viewing a work of art in a museum is improved by reading the accompanying label describing the artist, artistic period, medium, and some descriptive text, so a podcast listening experience is similarly enhanced by creating a text-based summary or introduction to the podcast. Podcast descriptions can include any or all of the following:

- The first names of the children who made the podcast (or their student number or "online nickname"—see Chapter 7 for more information)

- The grade level of the students

- The title of the podcast

- A brief description of the task and the process

- The equipment used

- Something in particular that the listener should be looking for

- The learning objectives met by the podcast

Following is an example of the text created to promote a current events podcast:

In this podcast, Jason and Chase went on location to the cafeteria to report about Mix-It-Up Day, a day when kids sit with groups of kids that they might not normally sit with. They interviewed kids and staff members to learn about the impact of this special event. They used a video iPod with a Belkin TuneTalk attachment to record their interviews and edited it using Audacity. Click here to hear their podcast.

To create the link, highlight the words "Click Here" and follow your Web authoring software's instructions to paste in the Web address, starting with http://. Publish the Web page, and the link is ready.

When users click on the link, they will be taken to a new screen, or their chosen default audio player will open, and the audio file will begin playing automatically.

Publishing work online and linking to it a Web site is useful for

- providing context and explanation for student work;

- sharing student work publicly;

- giving students a real-world audience and real-world motivation; and

- providing a master list of all podcasts on a single, easily skimmed Web page.

■ OPTION FIVE: UPLOAD THE FILE AND LINK TO IT ON A BLOG

This is a preferred method for organizing podcasts. While similar to the Web page option above, using a blogging platform offers more searchability, ease of use, and functionality.

WordPress blogs, as discussed in Chapter 1, are particularly appealing for podcasters. Edublogs (http://www.edublogs.org), a free blogging site for educators, is built using WordPress technology. Podcasts can be uploaded directly into a blog posting, so there is no need to acquire additional server space. Several blog templates are available, and some automatically embed the podcast right into the blog posting, so when users click on the link, the podcast plays without changing to a new window. The listener can play, pause, and adjust the volume of the podcast without leaving the blog screen. This is a tremendous advantage, as listeners can hear the podcast while reading the description of the podcast, keeping content and context together.

Another advantage of blogs over Web pages is that users can subscribe to the blog content using a blog aggregator such as Bloglines (http://www.bloglines.com), as described in Chapter 1. This allows parents and administrators to passively monitor educators' blogs and automatically have new content delivered to them. Users of blog aggregators like Bloglines never waste time visiting a blog that hasn't been updated. New content appears automatically, making a class blog a great way to integrate into parents' existing practice. It is more likely that people will actually follow your blog if they can do so passively.

■ OPTION SIX: ADD A PODCASTING FEED TO YOUR BLOG AND LIST IT IN A PODCASTING DIRECTORY

Subscribing to a Feed

RSS feeds also make it possible for podcasts to be automatically delivered to the user. Using a podcasting aggregator like iTunes, people can find your podcasts and subscribe to them. Just like subscribing to the local newspaper means finding it on one's doorstep each morning, subscribing to a podcast means new episodes automatically show up in the podcast aggregator. From then on, when a user opens iTunes, the software automatically "visits" all of the podcasting feeds to which the user subscribes and downloads new podcasts to the user's hard drive. The user can then listen to it via iTunes or transfer the files to an iPod (the downside of iTunes is that the iPod is the only mp3 player with which it interfaces).

Setting Up an iTunes Feed

iTunes allows any user to submit his or her RSS blog feed to iTunes for approval and inclusion in its catalog of podcasts. iTunes will automatically strip out the blog text and use the links to the podcast to generate audio content. While iTunes may be able to "guess" at a blog's feed, it may be more reliable to use a feed-creating Web site such as Feedburner to create the feed on your behalf. Then submit the Feedburner link to iTunes. Specific instructions for generating a podcast feed with iTunes are available at http://www.apple.com/itunes/store/podcaststechspecs.html.

To Feed or Not to Feed?

Because an RSS feed used by a podcasting aggregator delivers just the audio mp3 files to subscribers, not any text, it should be considered carefully. First, it may be that having an RSS feed open to anyone troubles district administrators. Conversely, being able to say, "Our podcast is available through iTunes" may provide a level of prestige that may appeal to an administrator.

To determine whether or not a podcast feed is right for your projects, consider these different scenarios. In the first scenario, a media specialist works with many different classes on many different projects. The projects vary in terms of style and genre. The media specialist decides that these podcasts need to be contextualized before someone hears them, which will not be possible in an iTunes feed, so she decides to post them to her blog instead, where parents can search by category to find what they are looking for. In the second scenario, a teacher works with a collection of students to develop a radio broadcast (see Chapter 12). Each week, the format of the show is relatively the same. In this case, the work does not need contextualization, and an iTunes feed is a logical alternative. If a feed is established, the instructors leading the project might want to periodically record their own podcast that reflects on past work and accomplishments.

■ Conclusion

As the technical preparations portion of this book draws to a close, it is time to build excitement and enthusiasm for launching podcasting in your own school. The next chapter offers suggestions for building a network of supporters for your program.

Chapter 7
Launching Podcasting in Your School

■ INTRODUCTION

Now that the practical steps of podcasting have been discussed in earlier chapters, you are ready to launch a podcasting project. This chapter serves as a road map for launching podcasting successfully in your building.

Educators' unique responsibilities for student safety, welfare, and learning require a few moments of reflection on how podcasting can and will fit in with the specific dynamics, curriculum, and staff of your building. Whether you are a teacher with domain over your own classroom, a resource room teacher providing support to many students in many classrooms, a media specialist in contact with the entire building, or somewhere in between, a few preparations will make your first podcasting projects go smoothly, with the endorsement of parents, colleagues, and administrators. This chapter explores some of the preparatory activities that will help shore up support.

■ DEVELOP A PROFESSIONAL LEARNING COMMUNITY

Seek out a handful of colleagues who agree to explore podcasting with you. They might be building colleagues or associates across the district, state, or country. Choose collaborative partners with whom you can be honest about missteps and celebrate accomplishments. Many of the ideas in this book come from discussions with colleagues and collaborators. An educator working alone has a single perspective. Five educators working together get five sets of experiences, feedback, perspectives, lesson plans, tips about grant funding, and more. Use e-mail, a wiki, or a discussion board to facilitate asynchronous discussion if there is no common planning time.

If possible, convene lesson review sessions among educators, with each educator presenting a podcasting project to the group, along with information about the lesson plan and desired outcomes. The other members of the group do not speak until the presentation is over. They then offer constructive feedback. Phrases from peers like, "I wonder what would be different if . . . " or "I wonder how students would react if . . ." help keep the tone positive rather than critical. Consider these four areas for reflection and evaluation:

- **Content:** the ideas, thoughts, and conclusions expressed during the podcast

- **Delivery:** the quality of speaking, sound effects, and musical choices

- **Production values:** clarity of recording, sound quality, microphone quality, skill of editing

- **Process:** quality of the steps and processes students used to move from the beginning to the end of the project

- **Instructional design:** the teacher-generated lesson plan and assessment strategies

Another option is to create a podcasting study group at the district or intermediate school district level. Seek a district administrator or building principal willing to fund a half-day brainstorming session or in-service. Be sure to document the group's findings on a Web page, via a free, password-protected Moodle discussion board (download Moodle for free at http://www.moodle.com) or by adding it to the Podcasting at School wiki (http://podcastingatschool.seedwiki.com). Alternatively, consider joining an educational technology organization or monitoring the online podcasts of other schools.

■ POLICIES AND PROCEDURES

Because most podcasts are placed on the open Web where anyone can access them, it is essential to develop guidelines for podcasting content and procedures for developing podcasts. These are useful not only in the classroom but for building administrative and parental support.

Student Policies

Consider the following questions prior to the first student podcast. The answers may depend on the particular school culture, age of students, and building policies and procedures.

- **How will students name themselves in the podcast?** Some elementary teachers assign a number to each student (giving the number 1 to the child whose last name comes first in the alphabet, the number 2 to the next student, etc.). Students label all of their papers, supplies, mailbox, and more with this number, and this number can also be used as their podcasting "name." Because students in the class are so familiar with the other students' numbers, they know the "real" identity of the podcaster, but the teacher has the confidence of knowing that her students' identities are safe online. Another option is to invite students to use their first names only; if there are multiple students with the same first name, they may choose a nickname. The students of the Downs FM radio podcasts in the United Kingdom give themselves a DJ nickname, referring to themselves with names like "DJ Bubbles" (http://www.downsfm.com). They even assign themselves an avatar (a graphic depicting themselves as a comic book character) on their Web site. In his blog, educational technology speaker David Warlick shared an idea for student privacy: use an anagram generator to scramble the letters of the students' last names for a clever, privacy-protecting nickname. He recommends the anagram creator at http://wordsmith.org/anagram (Warlick 2007).

- **How will I structure the assignment to keep kids anonymous?** Students should not be asked to share any personal details that might jeopardize their online safety, such as siblings' or friends' names; last names; references to streets or addresses; or religious or sports team affiliations. Therefore, an autobiographical writing assignment is not appropriate for podcasting.

- **How can I be sure they don't reveal something they shouldn't?** The safest way is to listen to each broadcast before it is posted online.

- **What content, language, or subject areas are off-limits for kids?** David Warlick (2006), in a presentation to the Michigan Association for Media in Education, addressed this question brilliantly. His solution? Refer to the student handbook. If foul language isn't permitted at school, it is not permitted in a podcast. If defamatory content is prohibited in the hallways, it is prohibited online.

- **May students make podcasts in the library? At home? Or only during class time?** This is more a question of the instructor's personal comfort level and the at-home resources of students. Many schools cannot afford to keep a set of equipment at school and have an additional set available for checkout. However, high school teachers may feel comfortable asking students to create podcasts from home using one of the free phone-in voice mail products.

■ PRACTICAL PROCEDURES

It is also important to consider practical management strategies for equipment and materials. This is especially crucial for staff members such as computer teachers and school library media specialists, who may be responsible for coordinating the activities and equipment needs of multiple teachers and classrooms. Following are suggestions that may help:

- **Establish a reservation/sign-out system for portable equipment.** Consider adding pages to an existing equipment sign-out book or establishing an online sign-out calendar. Add a bar code to portable equipment and add the item to the library inventory so it can be quickly checked out and tracked. Consider setting up a special "podcasting" item type in the circulation software with a one-day-only checkout time.

- **Design an equipment-sanitizing schedule.** If sharing microphones or headsets among several groups of students, consider how they will be kept germ-free, especially in winter months. Several companies now manufacture disposable antibacterial towelettes, generally found in plastic pop-top tubes in the cleaning section of grocery and discount stores. (An example is Clorox Wipes.) Another similar product that contains slightly less liquid content is sanitizing phone wipes, available at most office supply stores. Avoid window cleaner wipes unless they are specifically marked as sanitizing or antibacterial.

- **Host an informal in-service introducing staff to the new equipment.** A brief introduction and modeling during a staff meeting or in-service can pique the interest of colleagues, who can return to you at a later date for more specific training.

- **Create device-specific instructions sheets that circulate with the item.** Boost staff and student confidence by creating simple instruction sheets to accompany face-to-face instruction. Consider circulating portable items in clear, zipper-lock storage bags with instructions—or the URL for a great online tutorial—taped to the bag.

■ ADMINISTRATIVE SUPPORT

It is useful to gain the support of supervisors and colleagues prior to embarking on a podcasting project, especially if one's position within a school serves more than one classroom of students. Prepare a neatly formatted, one-page document about the benefits of podcasting to share with your administrator, department head, or district curriculum coordinator, and draft a parent permission slip (see next section).

For some administrators, the word "podcasting" instantly conjures up mental images of those iconic iPod silhouettes bopping and grooving to music. Be sure to frame any administrative proposal with a list of bullet points about the ways in which podcasting could be used to complement teaching and learning, so that the principal has a context for understanding the equipment use. Request a sit-down meeting to talk through administrative concerns. When administrators see proposals framed in terms of student content mastery, they are often more than happy to support the innovation.

■ GAINING PARENT PERMISSION AND SUPPORT

Many school districts ask parents to sign a blanket media permissions form that grants permission for the district to release a child's photo or likeness to the media. A student's work online should qualify under this permissions form. However, many parents are justifiably leery about their students' work being posted online, and a parent notification/permissions letter can do much to reassure them and build enthusiasm for their students' upcoming work.

Effective letters to parents should have six goals:

1. Explain the educational value and benefits of podcasting.
2. Give a brief overview of how podcasting will be used to meet curriculum goals.
3. Reassure parents about precautions that will ensure their children's safety online.
4. Direct them to the Web site or blog URL that will contain the links to the podcasts.
5. Give them an e-mail address, telephone number, and/or URL of a Web page where they can learn more.
6. Provide the permission slip for signature by parent and student.

Consider circulating the parent permission letter among staff and a few trusted parents to get feedback to the draft. Go over the letter with students prior to sending it home so that they can clearly articulate its content to their families. A sample permission slip is on page 60.

Date

Dear Parents and Guardians:

Podcasting is coming to our school! Podcasting is a growing technology trend that uses simple equipment to make audio recordings that can be burned to CD, posted to the Web, or downloaded onto an mp3 player. We find that podcasting improves student fluency, builds confidence, motivates quality work, and develops a real-world audience for student work.

We are beginning an **optional** lunchtime Podcasting Club for fourth graders. All interested fourth graders are invited to participate. Good effort and attitude are the only prerequisites for continuing beyond the first session. Each week, up to eight students will visit the Media Center for two lunchtime visits. They will eat lunch in the Media Center, then work on a podcasting project – perhaps a small research project, an interview, a radio play, or more! – that will be completed that week. The final products will be posted to the Web. Students will continue on a rotating basis. Because we cannot accommodate all interested students each week, we will use a lottery to choose the first participants. We will hold the lottery to choose the first students on
_____. Permission slips received after that date will be placed on the list in order of receipt.

By signing this permission slip, you give permission for your student to participate in the Podcasting Club. You also grant permission for his/her podcasts to be posted online or on CD. We will protect your student's privacy by not using last names or personal identifying details in our podcasts. You will be able to listen to podcasts by visiting this Web site online: http://_____.

If your student is interested in participating in the Podcasting Club, both you and your child must sign and return the bottom portion of this page. Please contact us if you have any questions.

Sincerely,

Teacher #1   Teacher #2

- - - - - - - - - - - - - - - - - - -

PODCASTING CLUB PERMISSION FORM

My student has my permission to participate in the lunchtime Podcasting Club on a rotating basis. I understand that his/her podcasts created may be published on the Internet, on CD, or placed on an mp3 player. I also understand that no last names or identifying personal details will be used in these podcasts.

Student's Name _____

Student's Signature _____ Date _____

Parent/Guardian Signature _____ Date _____

■ SHARING THE FINISHED PODCASTS

When the project is finished, send a half-page note home to parents to let them know that the podcasts are completed and available for listening online. This note was sent home to parents of first graders after some on-the-fly interviews with students about the conventions of nonfiction books:

Dear Family,

We have been making podcasts in the Media Center. A podcast is a voice recording where we tell something we have learned. We have been learning about the different elements we can find in nonfiction books. We hope you will go to http://_____ and click on "First Grade" under the Categories section so you can hear what we have learned!

Please leave us a comment telling us what you think! (No last names or personal details—help us stay safe online!)

Love, _____(space left blank so child can sign own name)

Keeping parents informed about their children's work is extremely effective. Parents enjoy the opportunity to share their children's work with friends and relatives around the globe. They enjoy seeing their child's work celebrated, the kids love to see their parents' comments, and community enthusiasm for podcasting continues to grow.

■ STARTING SMALL: PODCASTING CLUBS AND SMALL GROUPS

If at all possible, try to arrange for the first podcasting projects to be with small groups of students, rather than a whole-class initiative. Working with groups of 10 or fewer students, preferably in pairs, has several benefits:

- You gain a small team of experienced podcasters who can later help when you begin podcasting projects with a whole class.

- Because the group is small, you can more closely observe the process, identifying areas that need further instruction and clarification.

- You build a strong bond with students, which gives them confidence in trying something new.

- You can experiment with software, hardware, and equipment on a small scale before investing in a classroom, building, or district initiative.

In many buildings, a media specialist is an ideal staff member to lead this small group experimentation. For example, a colleague of mine hosted a handful of students for a restless study hall while the rest of their grade level went to band and orchestra practice. She decided to change this by creating an ad hoc podcasting group. When students arrive in the media center now, they check the podcasting bin for the topic of the day. They respond in writing to the prompt (which might relate to a favorite book or Battle of the Books, for example) and then make a podcast. Their podcasts excite their colleagues about library initiatives and keep them engaged and writing instead of antsy and in need of monitoring. What is especially pleasing about this arrangement is that now *all* fifth graders participate in a performance-oriented activity: band, orchestra, or podcasting.

The author's media center hosts a podcasting club for interested fourth graders. Each week, on a rotating basis, six to eight fourth graders come to the media center during their regular 40-minute lunch/recess time. Each week focuses on a different genre, theme, or topic. On the first day, over lunch, students discuss their individual interpretations of the topic. Because this is an outside-of-class-time club, some topics are noncurricular. Sometimes, in collaboration with the classroom teacher, the topic relates to their in-class learning. At other times, introducing a new piece of equipment or software is the focus. The small group creates an intimate learning environment. Past projects have included the following:

Genres

Interview of a colleague, character, historical figure, or animal

Interview "live from the scene" of a school event

Poetry and choral readings

Advertisements and commercials

Math quizzes

Weather reports

Personal essay/personal narrative (within the safety guidelines explained earlier in this chapter)

Mini-research projects

News reports "live from the scene" of a moment in history

Topics

School events and activities

Cooking/recipes

Current events from class

New Year's resolutions

Holiday traditions

Students, often working in pairs, brainstorm how they will interpret the theme. Often, a graphic organizer or worksheet helps them quickly organize their thoughts. The remainder of the first session is spent composing interview questions and answers; writing or choosing public domain poetry; writing persuasive, narrative, or informational text; or doing research to learn more about a given topic.

The first project for each student always involves Audacity, so that students gain basic mastery of the software before moving to more complex projects. Then they are ready to take a portable recording device outside the media center, conduct interviews, and transfer the footage to Audacity for editing. Given the brief time frame, each week can only incorporate one new skill.

The second lunch/recess period is for recording. During lunch, students review the plans for recording. They mark up their scripts, circling or highlighting key words that deserve extra emphasis or making marginal notes such as, "stop and breathe" or "pause here." Students then move to the computers and make a few practice recordings. The students relax when they know they have multiple chances to "get it right."

The podcasting club model is successful on many levels. First, it is extremely flexible. The small groups mean limited equipment is needed, making equipment and software experimentation easier. Potential future lesson plans can be tried and quickly abandoned if they are poorly designed or ineffective. The lessons learned can be extrapolated to large-group projects, and funds can be spent more meaningfully because equipment can be field-tested by this small group of students.

Students enjoy a chance to experiment as well. Especially with middle-grade students, the U.S. curriculum model rarely emphasizes performance-oriented projects. Podcasting literally gives voice and attention to students who might otherwise be academically average. Some students have been so motivated by podcasting club that they have taken on challenging research and pushed themselves to develop far more complex projects than they would have undertaken in the regular classroom. There is deep pleasure in watching students develop confidence and skill over time, listening to how their voices grow in animation and poise with each podcast.

While this podcasting club meets over lunch, it could just as easily meet during other times, such as

- during Drop Everything and Read (DEAR) time in a classroom (if the students are rotated each week, they would miss very little reading time);

- before or after school;

- as a subgroup pulled out during a scouting meeting;

- as a subgroup pulled periodically out of a secondary school's advisory program;

- as a public library youth or teen outreach program; or

- as a series of "Getting to Know Our School" interviews, coordinated by the principal in the main office.

Many other staff members can lead podcasting clubs. For example, a guidance counselor or social worker could work with students to develop a series of interviews about social issues and self-esteem. The school nurse could coordinate public health podcasts. A technology support staff member might be able to partner with students to create podcasts promoting the school's new Web site, software, or blog. The athletic director could pull a few students to write promotional podcasts for upcoming athletic events. Enrichment or gifted and talented staff could pull a small group of students from each class in a grade level for a podcasting session. The reading specialist could make recordings of students reading work aloud, developing a cumulative audio record of student fluency that becomes a part of a student's permanent record. When these recordings are shared with teachers throughout the building, they become ambassadors for podcasting as a relevant educational tool.

Finally, the most powerful small-group podcasting might be to begin by partnering with the special education department. These students often struggle with writing and reading. Because of their smaller caseload, resource teachers are ideal experimenters with podcasting. Many students with special needs struggle with reading and writing. Some dictate their work to a paraprofessional, who writes down their ideas on their behalf. While this helps students complete the assignment, many students—especially when they leave elementary school for secondary classrooms—feel socially stigmatized by the presence of a paraprofessional. If a student dictates into an iPod or hears his or her test read aloud on an mp3 player, he or she can gain greater independence and pride. Best of all, paraprofessionals no longer need to provide real-time support—they can transcribe the dictation at a time that is convenient for the staff. Administrators see a meaningful connection between podcasting and learning. And imagine the paradigm shift: the special needs students as the *first* to try the exciting new technology! Imagine how that would empower students and build pride among their parents and families. In addition, podcasting can awaken and motivate nontraditional students, as mentioned earlier, in remarkable ways. More resource room applications are covered later in this book.

■ CONCLUSION

A well-planned introduction to podcasting can help transform people's perceptions of podcasting from "fad" to "fantastic." Investing time in building support from colleagues, teachers, students, and parents can make the lesson plans presented in the next section of this book more promising and successful.

Part II
Ideas for Teaching and Learning with Podcasting

Chapter 8
Great Podcasting Lessons

■ INTRODUCTION

Now that the mechanics of podcasting have been established, this book turns to the ways in which podcasting can be used at school. This chapter shares more than 125 potential podcasting lessons. Some projects can be carried out with the few simple descriptive sentences here. Other lessons are described in further detail in the following chapters.

As you work with students to develop podcasting projects, please consider submitting them to the Podcasting at School wiki at http://podcastingatschool. seedwiki.com.

A

▶ *Activity Instructions at a Center*

In many elementary classrooms children circulate independently among a variety of learning stations. For children who do not yet read, consider recording the instructions for an activity as a podcast.

▶ *Advanced Placement*

High school Advanced Placement (AP) courses have rigorous syllabi. Students must not only master material as it is presented, but they must also recall that information on the end-of-year College Board examination to earn college credit. To prepare for the end-of-year exam, teachers can record their lectures throughout the school year and post them to a blog. Students can access the podcasts and leave their questions and responses using the blog's comments feature. Students who are absent can also access the lecture. As many universities are adopting podcasted lectures, this approach can be excellent preparation for college-level work. As an alternative to public blogging, consider setting up class accounts in an online learning system such as Blackboard or Moodle. These online class management systems provide space for uploading lectures, facilitating discussions, and more, in a password-protected environment to preserve the instructor's intellectual property.

▶ *Advertisements*

See Chapter 9.

▶ *Animal Reports*

Animal reports are common in elementary instruction. They are popular with students, and there are abundant age-appropriate resources available both in print and online. For first or second graders, consider a mystery guest animal report. Ask students to assume the voice of the animal they are researching (see Mystery Guest, p. 77). Using the first person, students might write a monologue describing the animal without naming it. Follow this format:

> Hi. I am (student's name)'s Mystery Guest. I am a (mammal, reptile, etc.). I live in (names of countries, states, or regions) in a (type of habitat). I eat (list food). My enemies are (list enemies). I look like this (give physical description). Some other interesting facts about me are _____. Can you guess who I am?

Play the final podcasts for the class. Early elementary students love to listen to each other's oral recordings and guess the animal.

▶ *Announcements*

In many schools, morning announcements are read over the public address system. Place podcasting equipment next to the P.A. system and record the announcements. Archive them on the school Web site so parents are informed about what is happening at school.

▶ *Artist Statements by Students*

Art curators create placards that hang next to works of art and explain the vision, materials, and/or creative process of the artist. After a project in any academic area, ask students to explain and reflect on the process of a project via a podcast.

▶ *Assessment*

Oral assessment can be a way of checking for understanding. Walk around the room as students are working in small groups. Conduct mini-interviews in each group to probe for understanding. Record the interviews for documentation or to share with students or parents.

▶ *Art Show Tours*

See Chapter 10, "Audio Tours."

▶ *Audio Tours*

See Chapter 10.

▶ *Author/Illustrator Interviews*

- If an author or illustrator is visiting school, designate one or two students to interview him or her on the day of the visit.

- Alternatively, ask the author or illustrator to participate in an interview prior to the visit via Skype (see Chapter 3).

B

▶ *Biographical Sketch*

Students choose a figure to research and create a dramatic monologue in the voice of that character.

▶ *Blogs That Talk*

Talkr (http://www.talkr.com) is an intriguing approach to podcasting. It is a plug-in addition for blogs. When a new blog entry is created, Talkr's software scans the text and automatically converts it into a computer-generated voice podcast. A link to the podcast appears automatically. The quality and fluency of the computerized voice is remarkable. Talkr can support schools in many ways. Educators who dislike the sound of their voices may prefer a machine voice. Administrators who keep a blog but are too busy to begin podcasting can now have audio created automatically. Early elementary students who are emerging or non-readers can enjoy blog content by hearing rather than reading it. Configuring Talkr can be time-consuming, but the benefits outweigh the hassle. See http://wordpress.org/extend/plugins/sds-talkr/ for details on configuring Talkr on a WordPress blog. For those who blog with Edublogs, the Talkr plug-in is pre-installed; follow the remaining instructions on the page to complete the configuration process.

▶ *Board of Education Meetings*

Some large school districts already broadcast their board meetings on the radio or via cable television. Because of the costs affiliated with these types of broadcasts, they have been out of reach for some smaller school districts. Consider podcasting the meeting instead. Use a microphone designed for large spaces, such as a Belkin TuneTalk or a Snowball.

▶ *Booktalks*

A booktalk is a brief advertisement meant to entice someone into reading the book in its entirety. Booktalks rarely last more than two minutes. They introduce the author, illustrator, and main characters, and begin to describe the plot. They do *not* give away the ending! Booktalk computer kiosks can be set up in a school library or media center or hosted on a school Web page or blog. Consider clustering links to student-created booktalks on a Web or wiki page by genre. See also Chapter 9, "Advertisements." For sample booktalks, visit http://www.nancykeane.com.

▶ Business Class

- To help students practice real-world job interviews, partner with local human resources (HR) departments. Ask for permission to record their real-world interview questions.

- Record students giving their practice answers. Place students in small groups and use the practice answers to generate suggestions for how to improve for the future. If partnering with local businesses, e-mail the interview podcasts to the HR department for professional feedback.

- For marketing classes, record a sample marketing "pitch." In small groups, evaluate the strengths and areas for improvement.

- Marketing students can create advertisements for real or envisioned products. See Chapter 9.

C

▶ Characters in Literature

Understanding the literary concept of point of view can be difficult for students. To help, ask them to choose a supporting character from a work of literature. At various points in the plot, ask students to podcast a monologue in the voice of that character. They can describe the actions of the story or respond to the plot.

▶ Class Presentations

Many assignments across the curriculum require oral presentations to the class. These presentations can be improved if students record their presentation rehearsals and then play them back, assessing vocal qualities such as speed, volume, and inflection. Recording the rehearsals also mandates that students rehearse, which is often missing from student preparations.

▶ Conference Attendance

- Take a portable podcasting device to conferences. When walking through vendor exhibits, dictate notes about items, books, and materials that you would like to investigate further upon return to school.

- Podcast workshop reflections for your colleagues who cannot attend. Either alone or with a partner, reflect on the two or three best ideas heard in a workshop as soon as the workshop ends. On the way home, review your podcasts and reflect on the day. Because these podcasts are short, their file size will be small. E-mail the podcasts to your colleagues the next day in lieu of writing a formal report.

- See also Professional Development (p. 79).

▶ Counseling/Social Work

Work with small groups to create a series of podcasts focusing on social issues such as bullying, cutting, healthy eating habits, self-image, or self-esteem.

D

▶ *Debate*

- Students engaged in debate rely on the quality of their content and the conviction of their presentation to make their case. Consider recording a sample debate and constructively critiquing it afterward.

- Partner with the coach of an opposing debate team to record a formal debate. Use the recording as an exemplar for future debate teams or for self-evaluation.

- In future rehearsals, excerpt portions of a debate and ask students to prepare a rebuttal.

▶ *Dramatic Monologues*

For students preparing monologues for a theatre and drama class, hearing themselves rehearse a monologue helps them develop self-evaluation skills in fluency, pitch, volume, speed, emotional intonation, and energy. If students are presenting monologues that are in the public domain, consider posting them online as a way to develop an online portfolio. Monologues that are still in copyright should not be posted online.

▶ *Driving and Thinking*

- Do you commute to work and think up great ideas while you drive? Take a portable recorder with you and dictate those great thoughts at a stop light. When you get to school, download the sound files and delete each file as you take care of that action item.

- On the way to work, record a daily message to post on your school Web site or blog. Make sure you are at a stop light first, and use a voice-activated recorder.

E

▶ *English as a Second Language/Limited English Proficiency*

See Foreign Language Applications (pp. 72–73).

▶ *Environmental Center*

Create a narrated tour of a nature walk for each season. Visitors can borrow an mp3 player from the park office by leaving their driver's licenses as collateral. Patrons play the audio files at their own pace, creating an individualized nature experience. See also Chapter 10, "Audio Tours."

▶ *Exchange with Other Classes*

A real-world audience can be a key to motivating students into making an extra effort. Consider exchanging student podcasts with another class. When students know that their peers will hear their work, their effort will improve, and so will the product.

▶ *Exemplar*

In teaching, it can be useful to have copies of model student work to share with classes. Consider recording outstanding oral presentations for use as exemplars. Ask future students to identify the elements of the oral presentation that make it outstanding (e.g., content, tone, volume, speed, and energy).

F

▶ *Family Tree*

Some middle school curricula contain a family tree unit. To be inclusive of adoptive or foster children, transform the project into a community tree—or community web—project and allow all students to think beyond blood relatives. Creating a community-focused tree or web lets students demonstrate their connectedness to mentors, favorite teachers, or friends. Consider adding oral interviews to the assignment. High school students could create a Web page that gives a graphic illustration of the tree or Web, with clickable links to the podcasts they have created. See also Chapter 14, "Oral History Projects."

▶ *Field Trip*

Portable podcasting equipment captures the best experiences of a field trip and shares them with families and the school community. Capturing the sounds of the fire station, recording an interview with a docent or the local baker, and interviewing peers about what they are learning on the field trip are all ways to share the field trip experience with others. See also Chapter 10 and Zoo (p. 85).

▶ *Folktales and Fairy Tales*

After a literature or media center unit on folktales, students write their own and record them. To add life and vibrancy to the recording, they can borrow drums, cymbals, chimes, xylophones, or other nonmelodic instruments from the music specialist. For this project, it may be useful to record two tracks. First students record the voice track, reading the story aloud into a headset. Then they unplug the headset and exchange it for a USB microphone on a stand. They return to the beginning of the podcast and add a new track with the instruments' sound effects.

▶ *Foreign Language Applications*

- In many foreign language classrooms, the teacher speaks new vocabulary aloud, and the class then repeats the words. Place a high-end recorder, such as a Snowball microphone or an iPod with a TuneTalk attachment, in the middle of the room and capture this dictation so students can practice pronunciation at home.

- Write dialogues that incorporate new vocabulary and record them. Distribute a printed version of the conversation as well as an audio copy on CD, a portable mp3 player, or the Web. Encourage students to mimic the accents and speech patterns of the dialogue to prepare for later presentation to the class. Hearing the dialogue also makes memorization easier and improves the students' accents.

- Partner with students in another country. Record brief messages in your student's native language (to keep the file size manageable) and e-mail them to class pen pals. Students in each country will hear the language they are learning spoken by children, not adults, as in most prepackaged foreign language curricula.

- Take a portable digital recorder on a trip and ask native speakers for permission to record their colloquial speech. Record each phrase as a separate podcast and link to them on the language department's Web page.

- Efficiently evaluate student fluency by recording a set of questions asked by the instructor to which students record their responses. Record each question, leaving a long pause between the questions. Export the file into mp3 format and place it in the Common folder or Out box (the server folder where students can select teacher-made templates, rename them, and save them into their own folders.) Students use Audacity to open the file and adjust Audacity's settings by going to FILE > PREFERENCES > AUDIO I/O and checking the box next to "Play other tracks while recording new one." When students begin to record, the teacher's questions will play back, and the students' answers will be recorded on a new track. When the recording is done, students can delete the teachers' track, edit out pauses, re-export to mp3, and deliver the finished podcast to the teacher via e-mail or the teacher's electronic drop box for evaluation.

G

▶ Graduation Ceremonies

Capture the speeches of a graduation ceremony and post them online for friends and family who could not attend. An oral recording of student presentations, such as those made by the president of the graduating class, the valedictorian, and the salutatorian, can be used as exemplars for future speechwriters or as gifts.

▶ Graduation Memories

Whether graduating from kindergarten, elementary school, middle school, or high school, leaving an old school behind is full of memories for students and parents. Consider setting up an oral history booth at the Senior All-Night Party or a graduation party and gathering the thoughts and good wishes of those in attendance. For more information on oral history interviews, see Chapter 14.

H

▶ Health Class

Students or teachers can create a set of public service announcements relating to the concepts in health class. For example, a podcast could focus on the basic steps of CPR. See also Chapter 9, "Advertisements."

▶ Historical Fiction Radio Play

See Chapter 13.

▶ History

- Create a radio play set during a particular period in history. See Chapter 13, "Radio Plays."

- Create a news broadcast set during a particular historical era or event. See Chapter 12, "Radio Broadcasts."

- Create World War II patriotic advertisements. See Chapter 9.

▶ Holocaust Studies

During a study of World War II and the Holocaust, identify Holocaust survivors in the local area. Assign small groups of students to collaborate to create interview questions and interview a survivor. See also Chapter 14 "Oral History Projects."

▶ Home Economics

Cooking shows are all the rage on television—why not take to the airwaves with a cooking show recorded in home economics class? Divide the class into teams of three to five students and invite them to create a cooking show with a collection of recipes that create a complete meal. For example, consider asking each team to come up with an appetizer, a main course, a side dish, and a dessert. Begin the podcast with an introduction and end with a cheerful closing (à la Julia Child's *Bon Appetit!*).

▶ Homework

Assign a student to record the night's homework assignment from the board. The podcast can be posted online so that absent (or absentminded) students can retrieve the assignment. Alternatively, the teacher can record himself or herself reading the directions aloud.

I

▶ Interview a Long-Distance Expert

Use Skype to record student interviews with experts. See also Chapter 3, "Equipment and Software."

▶ Interview, Planning An

If a special guest is coming to the classroom, or students will be conducting an interview outside the classroom, set up a podcasting station where students can stop by and record a question they'd like to ask the expert. The expert can record his or her answers during the visit.

▶ Introspection

See Journaling (p. 75).

J

▶ Jazz Riffs

In some jazz ensembles, students first master an expert's jazz riffs before inventing their own. The instructor can make a recording of the classic jazz riff for students to use as a model. Because the classic riff is someone else's copyrighted material, do not post the example online.

▶ Journaling

As writing across the curriculum has gained momentum, many subjects now employ a form of journaling—ranging from scientific to personal journals—as a way of encouraging students to reflect on the classroom experience. For students with special needs, consider allowing a podcasted journal instead. For classes with limited technology equipment, consider putting students in a rotation, with a different student providing the reflection each day. Scaffold the activity using the following template:

- Who are you?
- What class is this?
- What are the three most important concepts we learned today?
- What is the homework for tomorrow?

K

▶ Kinesthetic Activities

See Physical Education (p. 78).

L

▶ Lab Observations

During science experiments, students' hands may be busy pouring solutions, dissecting, or assembling objects for a physics lesson. A voice-activated portable digital audio recorder can record student observations, keeping hands free to work on the experiment. See also Science Experiments (p. 81).

▶ Language Laboratory

See Foreign Language Applications (p. 72).

▶ Library Media Center Orientation

See Chapter 10, "Audio Tours."

▶ Literature

- For a genre studies unit, create a radio play in that genre. See Chapter 13, "Radio Plays."

- Re-create a scene from literature as a news broadcast (see Chapter 12) or radio play (see Chapter 13).
- See also Personal Essay (p. 78), Play-by-Play Variation (p. 78), Poetry (p. 79), Story Dictation (p. 82), Story Structure (p. 82), Writer's Workshop (p. 85), and Writing Directions (p. 85).

M

▶ Math Facts

Some mathematical facts, such as multiplication tables, require rote memorization before they can be applied. Spend a class period asking students to invent study podcasts to help their peers learn. These can include the following:

- A math quiz, in which students read math problems for their peers to answer. For this type of quiz, students should leave a long pause after they read the problems so that the listener has time to calculate and write down the answer. (If more time needs to be added between questions after recording, use GENERATE > SILENCE in Audacity to add in more time.)
- A recording of the class reciting the multiplication tables.
- A mnemonic rhyme or poem that helps students remember a mathematical process.

▶ Mnemonic Raps

See Chapter 11.

▶ Monologue

A monologue is a dramatic speech made by a solo performer. "To Be or Not to Be," from Shakespeare's *Hamlet,* is perhaps the best known example. Ask students to assume the voice of a figure from history or literature and to create and record a monologue. Some sample monologue assignments follow:

- You are a soldier in George Washington's boat as he crosses the Delaware. What is going on in your mind?
- You are struggling to raise the flag at Iwo Jima. What are you thinking about?
- You have been asked by a friend to participate in the Boston Tea Party. Describe the experience to your spouse when you return home that evening.
- Select a character from the play *The Diary of Anne Frank* and create a monologue about what he or she is thinking at the end of the scene you have just read.
- Female characters in *Julius Caesar* are assigned little dialogue in the play. Select a female character from the play and invent a monologue for her.

See also Biographical Sketch (p. 69) and Characters in Literature (p. 70).

▶ *Music*

See Jazz Riffs (p. 75) and Playing Tests (p. 78).

▶ *Mystery Guest—Classroom Visitor*

Build enthusiasm and excitement for an upcoming visitor by asking him or her to record a mystery guest promotional spot. In the podcast (use Skype or ask the person to call into your Gcast account), the visitor should reveal some details about himself or herself and a hint about why he or she is are coming to the elementary classroom. For example:

> Hi. I am Thursday's Mystery Guest. I am related to someone in your class. I am coming to talk to you about the special things I do in my job. Here are some of the tools I need to do my job: a computer, money, a tall counter, and special papers. Can you guess who I am?

Play the recording the day before the visit and ask students to record their guesses on a folded piece of paper. See who can guess accurately!

N

▶ *Nature Hike*

See Environmental Center (p. 71).

▶ *Newsletter*

Many classrooms publish a weekly newsletter. Consider a radio broadcast (Chapter 12) or a podcast instead. Publish the newsletter online and burn it to CD for families without Internet access.

▶ *News Broadcast*

See Chapter 12, "Radio Broadcasts."

O

▶ *Oral History Projects*

See Chapter 14.

P

▶ *Parent–Teacher Associations/Organizations (PTAs/PTOs)*

Podcast the featured speaker at PTA meetings. Place the podcast online so parents who cannot attend can still be a part of the activities.

▶ *Parent–Teacher Conferences*

- Place a computer in the hallway with links to student work to keep parents engaged as they wait to meet with their child's teacher.

- Create an oral history station for parents and students to interact with one another. See Chapter 14.

▶ *Personal Essay*

Producer Jay Allison has revised the 1950s series *This I Believe* for National Public Radio. Celebrities and noncelebrities alike are asked to create a statement of approximately 350–500 words in which they share a belief, virtue, or life view that they embrace. In an interview on *The Diane Rehm Show,* Allison explained that two simple rules help guide users toward successful oral essays ("Jay Allison" 2006). First, the essay must focus on what the speaker believes, not on what he does *not* believe. For example, a successful essay might say, "I believe in the power of love," not, "I don't believe in hate." Second, the essay must not try to convince the listener to adopt the speaker's viewpoint. Words like, "You should," should not be present. The essay is not designed to be persuasive but to be revelatory. Due to the personal nature of these broadcasts, consult with students before posting them online. Detailed essay-writing tips are available online at http://www.thisibelieve.org/essaywritingtips.html.

▶ *Physical Education*

Many of the exercises and activities of a physical education class can be recorded and posted online so that students can extend their physical activity at home. Lower elementary students can hear instructions for how to skip, middle school students can recall square dance moves for the folk dance unit, and high school students can relax with yoga poses.

▶ *Play-by-Play Variation*

Many students love the world of sports, in which sports reporters excitedly describe what is happening during the game, who has the ball, who just made a goal, and more. This is known as *color commentary.* Bring history alive by inviting students to retell famous historical events—the murder of Caesar, the raising of the flag at Iwo Jima, the first day of integration at Little Rock Central High School—in a color commentary format.

▶ *Playing Tests (Instrumental Music)*

One time-consuming part of the instrumental music classroom is playing tests, in which students play one at a time for the instructor. This can pose difficulties for classroom management, as most instrumental music classes are much larger than traditional classes. Instead, place a computer or portable podcasting device in each rehearsal room. Ask each student to record his or her playing test, beginning the podcast with the name, the class period (or name of ensemble), the date, and the piece of music he or she is playing. By archiving the recordings, music teachers can track individual progress across the year. An alternative is to have students record their playing tests and then use their one-on-one time with the instructor to evaluate the recording. This shifts the individualized attention to discussions of performance quality.

▶ Poetry

Hold a contest for original poetry. The winning entries are recorded and placed on the school Web page. For large schools, divide the contest into genres: free verse, limerick, haiku, sonnet, and so forth.

▶ Principal's Message

- Many administrative messages are text-only on a Web page, making them inaccessible to early childhood students, students with limited English proficiency, and students with reading disabilities. Record the principal reading the letter aloud and place a link to the podcast next to the letter online.

- If the principal keeps a blog, consider installing the Talkr plug-in (p. 69). Once configured, the Talkr plug-in will automatically convert the text of the blog into a podcast.

▶ Professional Development

Place a podcasting microphone in the center of a discussion group to capture their thoughts for sharing with other teachers. See also Conference Attendance (p. 70).

▶ Public Service Announcements (PSAs)

See Chapter 9, "Advertisements."

Q

▶ Qualitative Research

Qualitative research relies on personal stories instead of numerical data. It often involves interviews or written essay responses. Consider acquiring a portable voice recorder that can hang on a neck lanyard. By having the recorder always at the ready, the instructor is prepared to capture student insights as they occur. Especially at the elementary level, students can give more detailed and elaborate responses orally than they can in writing. Oral responses can often be gathered more quickly than written responses.

R

▶ Radio Broadcasts

See Chapter 12.

▶ Raps

See Chapter 11.

▶ *Reading Fluency*

Beginning readers need to practice reading aloud. Ask students to practice their reading skills by reading into a podcasting microphone. Some children may feel more comfortable talking to a stuffed animal placed next to the microphone. Export each child's recording as a separate podcast. When exporting into mp3 format, use the title of the reading selection for "Title," the child's first name for "Artist," and the date of the recording for "Date." Use iTunes to manage the files. Pulling up the files by "Artist" will make an instant reading fluency portfolio across the school year. Pulling up the files by "Title" will let teachers see a cross-section of how each student performed on the same reading practice activity.

▶ *Rehearsals*

Practice makes perfect, the saying goes. Students can make a rehearsal podcast and then use the performance reflection sheet (p. 127) to self-evaluate.

▶ *Research Process Interviews*

As part of the research process, students converse with their teachers and media specialists about their progress. Whether these conversations are informal or a scheduled research conference, create concrete documentation of the process by podcasting the conversations. If posted online, these podcasts help parents gain a stronger sense of the higher-level thinking and collaboration occurring in the media center. The following questions may help guide the conversation:

- Where are you in the research process? (Refer to a specific research model if applicable.)

- Is your original research question still what you are pursuing, or is your research taking you in another direction? What direction is that?

- What can we do to help you?

- Are the resources you are using giving you the information you need?

- What new resources might help you move forward more efficiently?

- What do you need to do next?

- What worries you?

- What are you most excited about?

- Do you feel you are on track to meet the deadline?

▶ *Rites of Passage*

Interview students at important milestones in their lives: graduation, moving up to middle school, leaving kindergarten, getting their driver's license, etc. See Chapter 14 for oral history interview advice.

S

▶ *School Motto, School Song, School Prayer*

Remember your first pep assembly in high school? Did you know how to sing the school song? Did you know your school's motto? If attending a private religious school, did you know the school prayer? Help incoming students get a leg up by asking older students to record these as a podcast. Place a link on the school's home page or freshman orientation site.

▶ *School Tours*

See Chapter 10, "Audio Tours."

▶ *Science Experiments*

During science experiments, students' hands are often busy manipulating lab equipment. Teachers can record the steps of the experiment for students to listen to at their lab tables. See also Lab Observations (p. 75).

▶ *Science Laboratory Observations*

See Lab Observations (p. 75).

▶ *Shakespeare*

Assign each group in a class a scene or two from a Shakespeare play. Students rehearse, then record themselves performing the scene. Assemble the scenes in order to create an audio book of the play. See also Monologue (p. 76) and Chapter 13, "Radio Plays."

▶ *Show and Tell*

Show and tell is a beloved ritual of early elementary classrooms, as students bring in objects from home that have special meaning to them. These personal presentations are often missed by parents, who would enjoy the opportunity to hear their children speak about objects and activities they love. Consider recording show and tell presentations and burning them to CD as a gift to the parents at the end of the year.

▶ *Singing Telegrams*

Is a traditional book report or informational report wearing thin? Entrepreneurial students can create a singing telegram to share what they have learned.

▶ *Soliloquoy*

See Monologue (p. 76).

▶ *Speech Therapy*

- Record speech exercises so parents can practice at home with their students. Burn to a CD or write a grant to buy portable mp3 plays such as an iPod Shuffle for participating students.

- Use podcasting software to make archival recordings of students reading the same passage at different points in the school year. Use the recordings to assess progress and growth. Play them back at individualized education plan conferences (IEPCs) so that parents and team members can see what progress has been made.

▶ Spelling Test Make-Ups

Dictating a make-up spelling test is almost always an inefficient use of the teacher's time. When a child is absent, record yourself giving the test to the rest of the class. When the child returns, he or she can play it back on the computer and complete the test.

▶ Sponge Activities

"Sponge activities" are activities that keep students engaged and busy during the first few moments of class, when the teacher is preoccupied with attendance, collecting homework, or speaking with students. Consider prerecording dictations or brief quizzes that are played during "sponge" time. Examples: math facts, name the state capital, or dictate a letter and have primary students write it down.

▶ Sports Play-by-Play

Do your school sports teams regularly receive media coverage? If not, enterprising students can use portable podcasting recorders to create color commentary on the big game. See also Play-by-Play Variation (p. 78).

▶ StoryCorps Oral History Projects

StoryCorps travels the United States, capturing conversations between family members, some of which are broadcast on National Public Radio. To learn more about their techniques for taking oral histories, visit http://www.storycorps. net. See also Chapter 14, Oral History Interviews.

▶ Story Dictation

Some students spin vibrant improvisational tales aloud but struggle to put those thoughts on paper. Story dictation can be a useful solution. Encourage students to tell the story into the microphone. They can then transcribe what they wrote (or an instructor, paraprofessional, or parent volunteer can transcribe it for them) and use it as their first draft.

▶ Story Structure

- Understanding the structure of a story (exposition, rising action, climax, falling action, and resolution) can be difficult for students. Divide the class into five groups and bring them to the computer lab. Assign each group to a podcasting computer. Define exposition for the class (introduction of characters, setting of scene, etc.), then ask each group to record an exposition for a new story. After five minutes, each group shifts to a new computer. Define rising action, then ask them to listen to what has already been recorded and add the rising action for the story. Shift computers again, and repeat for each of the remaining steps. At the end, enjoy listening to the five improvised stories.

- *Alternative for younger students:* structure the assignment around three steps: beginning , middle, and end. Use words like, "the first thing," "next," and "finally" to focus students.

▶ *Students with Special Needs*

- Students with special needs who have difficulty with handwriting or typing, and who usually dictate to a paraprofessional or teacher, can use podcasting software to give dictation privately. The dictation is later transcribed by a paraprofessional for the student to review. Being able to work independently, without a support staff member nearby, can help to develop the esteem of secondary students in particular.

- Some students' individualized education plans (IEPs) mandate that tests be read aloud. Record the test as a series of podcasts. To make navigation easy for the student, make each section of the test its own podcast, and use the "Title" field to describe that section (e.g., "Multiple Choice, 1–15").

- Assign digital voice recorders to older special needs students. Make arrangements with classroom teachers for them to record lectures to facilitate studying for tests. Consider a parent permission slip so that the school is protected against loss or theft. Choose a digital voice recorder, such as those in the Olympus series, that has small holes at the top so that it can be worn on a lanyard and won't be misplaced.

- See also Speech Therapy (p. 81).

▶ *Summer Reading Program*

Looking for a way to keep students motivated throughout the summer reading program? Set up an RSS feed and publish a weekly podcast just for them! Include book talks, set mini-goals, and celebrate the achievements of productive readers.

T

▶ *Tech Tips*

Some students and educators struggle with mastering the steps of a particular technology software or process. A skilled student or educator can record instructions that the user can play back. Alternatively, the technology department of a school or district can record a regular podcast, with each episode featuring a new piece of technology equipment, software, or Web-based application.

▶ *This I Believe*

See Personal Essay (p. 78).

▶ *Time Capsule*

It is common for a time capsule to be buried in the foundation of community buildings. The time capsule is a sealed container featuring artifacts from the present day that would help future residents understand the daily life of community residents. If a new school, library, town hall, or community center is being built, conduct oral history interviews (see Chapter 14) to gather citizens' memories of the old facility, and deposit a CD or inexpensive mp3 player into the time capsule. (Avoid putting batteries in the time capsule, as they may corrode over time.)

▶ *Tours*

See Chapter 10, "Audio Tours."

U

▶ *Understanding the Research Process*

See Research Process Interviews (p. 80).

V

▶ *Veterans' Interviews*

The Library of Congress's American Folklife Center runs the Veterans History Project, which seeks volunteers to lead oral history interviews with veterans and civilians. Learn more about oral history projects in Chapter 14, or visit http://www.loc.gov/vets for extensive information about planning, leading, and submitting an interview to the project.

▶ *Vocal Exercises*

A choir or theater director can record warm-up scales, songs, or tongue-twisters for students to practice at home.

W

▶ *Walking Tour*

See Chapter 10, "Audio Tours."

▶ *Welcome to My Class*

Children cannot wait to learn about their new teacher. Early childhood teachers can record an audio welcome for incoming students and post it online. For small classes, the welcome could be customized for each student. Alternatively, the teacher's welcoming podcast could be burned to an audio CD and mailed in the children's welcome packets, along with recordings of some of the songs, chants, mottos, and phrases that they will use in class.

▶ *Writer's Workshop*

One of the areas in which young writers struggle is revision. Students have difficulty identifying their own errors in word choice, punctuation, or spelling. In addition, young students often think that once they have finished writing their work down, their work is complete. Podcasting equipment is an unexpected ally in the writing process. As students read their work into a microphone, they often stumble over their mistakes, discover a less awkward way of expressing themselves, and catch syntax errors. When used during the writing process as an editing tool, the podcasts themselves are discarded, as the goal is to assist in the revision process only.

▶ *Writing Directions*

Many writing teachers use a lesson that requires students to write directions. Students must think explicitly about a task, breaking it down into the exact steps required to complete it. Ask students to write the directions for a common household task (e.g., making a peanut butter sandwich, brushing teeth, starting a load of laundry, or washing the dishes), being careful to note *each step in the process*. If making a peanut butter sandwich, for example, simply saying, "Get bread," would be incomplete, whereas the following would be complete: "Untwist the tie that holds the bread bag closed. Take out two pieces of bread and put them on the plate. Reseal the bag." When the students have recorded their podcasts, set up several playback stations and invite the rest of the class to cycle through the stations, attempting to complete each task using *only* the dictated directions.

X

▶ *eXit Interviews*

At the end of a class or lesson, stand at the door with a portable podcasting device and ask each student to contribute one thing he or she learned during the lesson. Post the list online for students to review prior to a test.

Y

▶ *Yoga Poses*

See Physical Education (p. 78).

Z

▶ *Zoo*

During many elementary trips to the zoo, parent volunteers guide a small sub-group of students through the zoo exhibits. Give each group a portable voice recorder. At each stop, the parent asks a different child to give a brief summary of what he or she sees. To elicit responses that go beyond, "We're at the polar bears. They're cool," encourage students to respond to each habitat using each of the five senses (hear, taste, touch, smell, see).

■ CONCLUSION

Podcasting reaches all learners. The following chapter outlines how students can create a very short beginning podcast: an advertisement.

Chapter 9
Advertisements

■ INTRODUCTION

When first embarking upon podcasting as an educational tool, it can be tempting to envision a lengthy, multipart podcast, featuring music, multiple voices, and a series of segments edited together. However, a simple 30-second advertisement is much easier. Students enjoy creating advertising podcasts because the format allows them to take on an "adult" voice, which is often motivating and enjoyable. Teachers enjoy the format because it takes little time to prepare and is a natural opportunity to focus on persuasive writing and delivery, an important area of the writing curriculum. Because the content of an advertisement is so compact, it frees up time in the instructional design to teach students the basics of the podcasting process.

■ TYPES OF ADVERTISEMENTS

Advertisements generally fall into two general categories: consumer advertising and public service announcements (PSAs). *Consumer advertising* encourages the listener to buy a product. Therefore, its goal is primarily to persuade. It may employ devices such as skits, dramatic reenactments, sound effects, or atmospheric music to promote consumer goods and services such as automobiles, insurance, household products, or for-profit tourist destinations.

A *public service announcement,* on the other hand, is often provided by the radio station at no charge or at a significantly reduced cost because the content will benefit the public. These advertisements are also persuasive, although they focus on changing the listener's behavior rather than encouraging the purchase of a good or service. PSAs encourage the listener to believe in or take action in support of an issue. PSAs often focus on issues of public safety or good. Common subjects for PSAs include

- the importance of wearing a seat belt,
- the importance of properly installed child safety seats,

- the value of regular health screenings and immunizations,
- fire safety reminders,
- traffic safety hints, and
- Department of Homeland Security advice.

PSAs are often commissioned by government or not-for-profit organizations, whose advertising budgets are much smaller than those of for-profit corporations. In many cases, they feature a single voice and try to condense as much material into the announcement as possible. Use of music, dramatic skits, and multiple voices is uncommon.

■ POTENTIAL USES IN K–12 EDUCATION

Student-created advertisements can be used in a variety of ways in K–12 education. If time permits, it can be useful to bring in a professional advertising writer prior to beginning the project. Most major cities have advertising agencies who might be willing to send an employee to the school to discuss the creative process for advertisement creation. If a big-city advertising agency is not available, consider contacting local television and radio stations. Most of these stations have an advertising representative or "rep" whose primary function is to sell advertising time. In addition, they sometimes work with clients to write and publish the content. An advertising professional can provide a real-world perspective on the elements of advertising, which grounds the student's project in a meaningful context.

Student-created advertising activities could include the following:

School life

- Sell tickets to the prom, the school musical, a poetry slam, the school store, an athletic event, or a school social activity.
- Take a field trip. Then create a promotional advertisement for the destination.
- Encourage students to join a school club such as student council, Model United Nations, yearbook, forensics, or business club.
- Explain and support the school dress code or other school policies.

Literature

- **Shakespearean advertisements.** Many high school Shakespeare units discuss the price of a ticket to the Globe Theatre versus the price of a glass of beer or other common purchases. After researching items available for sale during Shakespeare's time, students create an advertisement to "sell" an item.
- **Shakespearean plays.** Students imagine themselves as Elizabethan theater directors and create advertisements promoting the world premiere of the Shakespearean play being studied in class.

- **Fantasy books.** Create advertisements for the fantastical products in such books, such as the candies in Willy Wonka's factory in *Charlie and the Chocolate Factory*.

- **Booktalks.** Librarians and school library media specialists often promote books through booktalks, which are brief, enticing commercials for quality books. Encourage students to create their own booktalks that spike the reader's interest but do not give away the ending!

- *The Scarlet Letter* (Nathaniel Hawthorne). Students assume the voice of Reverend Dimmesdale and create a pro-abstinence PSA.

- *Nothing but the Truth* (Avi). Students write a PSA about the importance of free speech.

- *The Misfits* (James Howe). Students write a PSA about the importance of respecting those of diverse backgrounds and beliefs.

Grammar and writing

- Reinforce student understanding of a grammatical rule or writing convention by asking them to create an advertisement for a fictional product that uses the rule a given number of times. As an example, use 10 prepositions to sell an amusement park: "Come *to* our park. Go *up* the Tower *of* Doom! Buy ice cream *from* our shop!"

- To explore simile, a sample assignment might be, "When I get up in the morning, the first thing I want is Raleigh's Rollos! They make me feel *like a world-class athlete!* They're *as round as a hula hoop! As nutritious as fresh fruit!*"

- Advertisements can also be configured to reinforce the format of a formal paragraph (topic sentence, three detail sentences, and a concluding sentence).

Social studies

- Sell Henry Ford's Model T, Madam C. J. Walker's beauty products, the Wright Brothers' bicycle, or another well-known invention from American history.

- Create a "Rock the Vote"–style advertisement explaining why citizens should register to vote and become involved in their community.

- Write World War II–era PSAs that stir up American patriotism and encourage the purchase of Victory Bonds, the establishment of Victory Gardens, the donation of scrap metal, the work of women in war plants, or other activities in support of the war effort.

Community and cultural life

- In conjunction with school visits from firefighters and police officers, create ads promoting fire safety, traffic safety, seat belts, or child safety seats.

- Promote disaster preparedness with PSAs discussing safe behaviors in a tornado, hurricane, or flood; community evacuation plans; or contents of a family emergency kit.

- Promote an upcoming museum, garden, or community center event or exhibition.

Science

- Promote science lab safety.

- Share fun and safe experiments to conduct at home using household ingredients.

Physical education and nutrition

- Promote the importance of daily fitness activities.

- Explain and promote the revised USDA "Food Pyramid."

- Create a series of nutritional PSAs focusing on various aspects of healthy eating (e.g., healthy snacks, components of a healthy breakfast, foods to pick for lunch in the cafeteria).

▉ PLANNING AN ADVERTISING PODCAST

Students may work alone or with a partner on this project. Because of the brevity of the recording, groups of more than two students are not recommended. In most cases, this assignment can be accomplished in two class periods. During the first class period, students brainstorm a topic, create the outline, and begin writing the script. During the second session, students complete the script and make the recording

Step One: Picture It

To envision an advertisement, students begin by understanding the type of advertisement they will create. This can be decided in advance by the teacher or, in some cases, by the students themselves. Students then work to brainstorm the focus of their advertisement and the key audience for their advertisement (peers, parents, community members, etc.). The evaluation rubric on page 91 can be used to help students envision what is expected of them.

Name _____

Advertisement
Evaluation Rubric

For each section, 1-10 points will be given. 10 is the highest possible score. The student will self-evaluate. The instructor will also evaluate the project and assign the final grade.

	STUDENT SCORE (1-10)	INSTRUCTOR SCORE (1-10)
ADVERTISING CONTENT		
The introduction "hooks" the listener.		
The middle sentences provide strong reasons to support the ad.		
The advertisement has a memorable ending.		
The script follows grammar and spelling conventions.		
RECORDING AND DISTRIBUTION SKILLS		
The student navigated the software with little teacher intervention.		
There are minimal errors, pauses, "um's," and "ah's" in the podcast.		
SPEAKING SKILLS		
The words are spoken clearly and are easy to understand.		
The podcast is performed with energy and enthusiasm.		
The podcast is easy to hear when played back.		
WORK SKILLS		
Time was used wisely.		
SUBTOTAL:		
TOTAL POINTS (OUT OF 100):		

COMMENTS

Step Two: Plan It

In the planning stage, students flesh out their ideas, adding supporting details and organizational structure. At their simplest level, advertisements are structured much like formal paragraphs. They begin with a topic sentence that "hooks" the listener and introduces the topic of the advertisement. Language is carefully chosen to pique the interest of the listener and can often appear in the form of a question. Introductory phrases in the form of a question are particularly popular among emerging writers at the elementary level. Examples of student introductions include the following:

"Have you heard about the new _____?"

"Have you ever wished you could _____?"

"Have you ever wanted to _____?"

"Did you know _____?"

"Last year, in our state, over _____ people _____ because of _____."

"You can help improve the world around you by _____."

Next come three to five sentences that support the topic. They provide more information, give examples, quote statistics, and give other reasons why the listener should take action in support of the topic or buy the product.

The advertisement ends with a summation. Like the opening sentence of the advertisement, the summation or conclusion harnesses powerful, memorable language to leave a lasting impression on the listener. Some students enjoy modeling their ending thoughts by creating a jingle. A *jingle* is a brief sentence set to a catchy tune. Jingles help the ad's message linger in the mind of the listener.

Whether the advertisement ends in song or spoken words, it should reinforce the message of the advertisement by mentioning the product ("Next time you're in the grocery store, choose Raleigh's Rollos!"), service ("When you need an oil change, consider Michigan Quick Oil Change."), or desired action ("Vote this Thursday.").

The worksheet on page 93 can help students outline the content of their advertisement.

Name _____

CREATE A RADIO ADVERTISEMENT!

What is a radio advertisement?
A 30-second recorded commercial that encourages the listener to:

Buy your product.	Support your cause.	Change their behavior.
"That's why you should try Chocolate-Covered Oreos!" "4 out of 5 dentists recommend Trident to their patients who chew gum!"	"Give money to the Salvation Army, so everyone can have a good holiday season." "Support the school playground fund!"	"Buckle up and stay safe." "Look both ways before you cross the street." "Brush your teeth after meals." "Make sure you get a flu shot."

What are you interested in writing a commercial about?

What is the catchy beginning you are going to use to "hook" your listeners and get them interested in your topic?

What are the most important ideas you need your listener to learn about your topic?

1. _____

2. _____

3. _____

4. _____

5. _____

What memorable ending will you use so that your listener remembers your message?

Bring this outline to your teacher to conference about it before you write up your script.

From *Podcasting at School* by Kristin Fontichiaro. Westport, CT: Libraries Unlimited. Copyright © 2008.

It is almost always preferable to have students create a script instead of speaking off-the-cuff from an outline. (An exception might be for drama, forensics, or other lessons that emphasize impromptu speech.) Once an outline is complete, students write out a script, using large, legible letters, double-spacing the text for reading ease. Only one side of the paper is used so that the paper does not need to be flipped over, the unwanted sound of which would be captured during the recording process.

Step Three: Record It

Before recording, students should relax and warm up their voices. See Chapter 4 for warm-up activities, which not only prepare the voice but relax the anxiety of nervous students.

When recording an advertisement, any kind of podcasting equipment or software is appropriate. Make sure the script is set down on the table instead of held in the students' hands. This minimizes shuffling noises that podcasting's sensitive microphones might pick up.

Encourage students to record the entire advertisement without stopping. The professional radio and television industry refers to each attempt to record something as a "take," as in, "Take 3!" Instead of editing together several "takes" for an advertisement, it is more efficient to have a student re-record an entire advertisement. This is also good instructional scaffolding if this project is the first in a series of podcasting projects. Save more sophisticated podcasting skills, such as editing or multiple tracks, for later projects. For this advertising assignment, keep the focus on quality content, persuasive writing, and podcasting basics.

Step Four: Edit It

If there are technical problems, such as issues about volume, distracting background noise, or clarity, encourage students to re-record their advertisement.

Step Five: Review It

The reviewing process is reflective. Students are encouraged to take responsibility for judging their work. As shown in the podcasting process illustration on page 9, the reviewing step is a chance to reflect prior to completing the process. It is useful to build review time into the work process and not to wait until the end of the project, when it may be "too late" to revise the project.

The assessment rubric on page 91 is a useful tool to guide students through the process of self-evaluation, Guiding students into self-reflection before turning in an assignment is an important step for developing strong, independent learners and creators of content.

Three possible outcomes might emerge from this self-evaluation:

• The project is complete, meets the assignment objectives, and is ready to be submitted.

- The content is complete, but there are vocal or technical errors that require the project to be re-recorded. The student should consult with the instructor(s) for advice on improving the sound quality or oral delivery of the content, then re-record.

- The project is technically competent, but there are weaknesses in the content that require parts or all of the project to be re-recorded. The student should consult with the instructor(s) or collaborative community partners for guidance on how to deepen and enrich what has already been accomplished, rewrite the script, and re-record it. (See the illustration on page 90.)

When the student and instructor agree that the project is complete, move to the next step.

Step Six: Distribute It

To showcase these advertisements, three distribution options are recommended. One is to insert the advertisements between segments of a longer radio broadcast (see Chapter 12). For example, if a middle school produces a broadcast, it could feature advertisements created by the elementary schools. Another is to publish them as freestanding advertisements on the school's Web space. A third option is to partner with local radio stations and ask if they will broadcast the students' work. If this option is chosen, be sure to check with the radio station in advance for the preferred file format for export.

CONCLUSION

The brevity of advertisements makes them a perfect introductory podcasting project. As students use advertisements to gain confidence and mastery over speaking, recording, and manipulating podcasting software, they will quickly be ready to move on to more complex projects such as the audio tours in the next chapter.

Chapter 10
Audio Tours

■ INTRODUCTION

For decades, art museums and special exhibitions have enhanced the gallery experience by offering audio tours of various exhibits. These tours choose significant works in each gallery room and give the museum visitor in-depth information about the selected works of art. They often invite the audience to examine particular aspects of a work or to compare it to another work. Sometimes the tour is available in two different formats: a children's version and a more advanced adult version. By marrying aural learning with the visual experience, the museum exhibitions educate as well as entertain.

Similarly, an audio tour can be a useful learning tool in K–12 education. Tours can be made by students as a way of exploring content and showcasing what has been learned, or they can be made by educators or other community adults as a way of transmitting information orally to enhance a field trip or help students orient themselves to a new environment.

Human-led tours require all learners to travel as a group. Audio tours are appealing because they differentiate, allowing each listener to acquire content at his or her own pace. Those in the back of the group may have difficulty hearing or seeing the content.

■ POTENTIAL USES FOR AUDIO TOURS IN EDUCATION

There are many potential uses for audio tours in the K–12 educational setting, including the following:

Student-Created Projects

- **Student-led school tours.** Some schools offer student-led tours to special guests and prospective students. Encourage a student tour guide to create an audio tour for the school. Invite community members to exchange their driver's licenses for an inexpensive mp3 player and take a self-paced tour of the school through the eyes of its students. This tour can also be made available to incoming freshmen or new high school students, who may wish to "look cool" by avoiding a formal school tour but still need to know where the school store is, where to go to find out about graduation requirements, and where the bathrooms are. (School security policies may preclude posting school tours online.)

- **Student art show tour.** Invite advanced art students to create an audio gallery walk. The students confer with the art teacher to select exemplary works. At each stop on the tour, students explain the learning objectives for that work of art and help the visitor see how those goals were brought to life artistically.

- **Student-created tour of a local attraction.** Some historical sites, botanical gardens, museums, history centers, parks, or interpretive centers would be interested in posting an audio tour on their Web site but lack the resources or staffing to do so. Partner students with historical sites or organizations. Students and site staff collaborate to identify the most important features of that particular place and then create an audio tour. This real-world application of student learning can be particularly motivating for students. Many organizations are interested in funding this type of school–community partnership.

- **Local history tour.** Many districts have a local history curriculum unit. As part of this unit of study, students visit the most important sites affiliated with their community. At each stop on the field trip, ask students to record the key features of that location based on the information presented by their guide. The results will demonstrate student understanding. An alternative approach would be for older students to create the tour for younger students, perhaps partnering with local history experts as discussed above.

- **Civilizations of the past.** Ask students to bring history alive! Using historical maps and primary source reference materials, invite students to create an audio tour of a historical fort, a Civil War battlefield, or ancient Athens or Rome.

- **Oregon Trail tour.** Many students study the Oregon Trail. Invite them to learn about the stops on the Trail in more depth as they create a virtual tour of many of the most popular stops along the way.

- **Historical neighborhood tour.** Many urban areas have historic districts containing homes that belonged to notable citizens of that community, and many civic organizations host holiday home tours to cover their operating costs. Prepare a podcast of the audio tour and distribute it on CD. Listeners can play the CD back in their cars as they travel between sites. For many years, the Memphis Inter-Faith Assocation (MIFA) hosted an elaborate holiday lights driving tour set in a local park. Upon payment of admission, visitors received a CD of local ensembles playing holiday music to accompany their tour of the lights. Why not partner with a vocal or instrumental music teacher and record their ensemble's performances for use as incidental music between tour stops or underscoring the narration? Include publicity information about your school and the charity at the conclusion of the

CD. (Be sure to seek appropriate permissions if recording and sharing musical arrangements that are still under copyright protection.)

- **Park tour.** This is another audio tour that could be distributed on CD and played back in cars, and such tours have been available in many of this nation's best-known national parks for many years. Different recordings could be made depending on the season so that visitors can learn about the types of animals, foliage, flowers, and tree growth available at that time of year.

Audio Tours Created by Adults for Student Use

- **Science lab safety tour.** Many science curricula include an orientation to the science laboratory. Create an audio tour in which students visit each of the lab's important stations, including the eye wash station, sinks, Bunsen burners, gas spigots, and more. Include important safety tips and rules. At the conclusion of the tour, hand students a brief assessment to check for understanding.

- **Media center orientation.** Many secondary media centers schedule orientation sessions with incoming students. Distribute mp3 players and invite students to interact with various sections of the library independently. Possible stops on the tour include location of the checkout desk, copy machine, and pencil machine; reference; nonfiction; fiction; maps and globes; magazines and periodicals; new book displays; and computer stations (include information about logging on and acceptable use). Invite students to follow the audio instructions for logging on to a computer station and have them follow your instructions for a sample search in a selected online encyclopedia, database, or Web site. They can record their answers on a simple worksheet. In between tour stops, share some of the library's special features, such as audio books, book clubs, open times for studying, and more. Imagine the "cool factor" the library will have when it hands out mp3 players!

- **Field trip audio tours with soundscapes.** Just as in the student-created tours above, educators can ask host sites for permission to visit the location in advance and create a podcast for students. Include an interview with gallery, museum, or site staff about important works and historical context. Insert questions into the tour and ask students to provide the answers in their field trip notebook. Create a *soundscape*—an audio collage of various sounds—for the beginning of the tour that helps students get into the mood of the location. For example, for a trip to a zoo's aviary, prerecord some of the bird sounds. For a trip to Colonial Williamsburg, find a podcast-approved recording of music of the period. For a visit to a Civil War battlefield, include the sound of cannons being fired.

■ PLANNING AN AUDIO TOUR PODCAST

Whether teachers create a tour for the purposes of transmitting information to students or students create them to demonstrate understanding and learning, the same podcasting process applies.

Step One: Picture It

In this stage, the creator "begins with the end in mind." He or she visualizes the final product, then considers the various steps that will be needed to realize that vision. These questions can guide the envisioning of the final product:

1. **What is the subject, focus, scope, or location of the tour?** The first question to consider is obvious: What will the audio tour be about? Where is the tour located? What special transportation arrangements and permission slips might be needed if the tour will be created by students? Consider scope and focus as well. For example, there is a significant difference between a general tour of Zion National Park and one that focuses only on a particular hiking trail within Zion.

2. **What equipment or software will be used?** Portable equipment works best for this project. An iPod with a TuneTalk attachment or an Olympus digital audio recorder that connects to a computer via USB would be ideal. If these are not available, a laptop on a cart with a headset is a slightly less portable solution. Recording via cell phone to a Gabcast account (http:// www.gabcast.com) or Gcast (http://www.gcast.com) is also an option. Some cell phones, such as the LG Chocolate Phone from Verizon, function as audio recorders whose files can later be downloaded for editing onto a desktop or laptop computer.

3. **Who is the intended audience?** An audio tour's content should be customized to fit the intended audience. For example, an audio tour through a sculpture garden for visitors with vision impairments would include a vivid description to help the person visualize the work of art. The podcast might also encourage visitors (with the garden's permission) to touch the sculpture to feel for particular details and textures. A podcast designed for a senior citizen tour bus group might be limited by the amount of time the bus will be stopping at a site. A tour of Boston's Freedom Trail for an Advanced Placement U.S. history course could incorporate quotes from primary source texts to help students connect the physical location to the historical background they will need for the end-of-year test. A tour of the same trail for elementary children would narrow the content down to the most important facts and might include learning devices such as short audio skits to transmit content.

4. **How will the podcast be distributed?** Audio tours can be shared with audiences in many ways. If funding permits, visitors might be loaned an easy-to-use mp3 player with the podcast loaded onto it. Geeks.com is a good source for closeout mp3 players at bargain prices. A less expensive option might be to burn the podcast to CD and distribute portable CD

players instead. Some visitors might be able to download the tour from a Web site and play it back on their own device. CDs enrich driving tours.

5. **Who are the project partners?** An audio tour can be created by a single person, or it can represent the work of a larger group. Group members might be other students, faculty members, or representatives from local cultural sites. Record the names and contact information for each participant.

6. **What is the timeline for the project?** A key to any successful project is a sense of the timeline of the project. Especially for students, break the project down into several smaller steps, each with its own deadline. Student-led tours benefit from these small deadlines because they provide many opportunities for student-teacher conferencing throughout the project.

7. **How will this project be evaluated?** If this will be a student-created podcast, what will they need to accomplish to achieve a good grade? The audio tour rubric, found on page 102, can serve as a guide for students.

The Audio Tour Project Map, found on page 103, is an easy way to document all of this information on a single page. A three-ring binder or three-pronged paper notebook can be useful to keep all project materials, including the project map, together and organized.

Step Two: Plan It

The planning stage is a practical stage during which the tour stops are chosen and sequenced, facts are researched, and a working script is created. During the planning stage, it is important to visit the tour site several times (unless creating an audio tour for an ancient culture as an exercise). Brainstorm all of the possible tour stops using the Audio Tour Brainstorming Sheet on page 104, then narrow the number of stops to a manageable number. Determining the number of stops may depend on the developmental age of the podcast creator and the audience and the amount of time available to complete the project, as well as the needs of the community partner.

Name _____

Audio Tour:
Evaluation Rubric

For each section, 1-5 points will be given; 5 points is the highest. The student will self-evaluate. The instructor will also evaluate the project and assign the final grade.

CONTENT OF TOUR

	STUDENT SCORE (1-5)	INSTRUCTOR SCORE (1-5)
The introduction is welcoming and friendly.		
The introduction tells where the tour will take place.		
There are at least three stops on the tour.		
The information provided for each stop is accurate.		
The information provided for each stop is engaging and interesting.		
There is a minimum of 3 pieces of information for each tour stop.		
There are directions to the next stop each time.		
The conclusion thanks the listener for taking the tour.		
The conclusion includes a book and/or Web resource related to the tour.		

RECORDING AND DISTRIBUTION SKILLS

The student navigated the podcasting software successfully.		
There are minimal errors, pauses, "um's," and "ah's" in the podcast.		
The document was successfully saved and exported to mp3 format.		

SPEAKING SKILLS

The words are spoken clearly and are easy to understand.		
The podcast is performed with energy and enthusiasm.		
The words are spoken at a relaxed, leisurely pace.		
The podcast is easy to hear when played back.		

WORK SKILLS

Deadlines were met on time.		
Time was used wisely.		
The student participated in conferences throughout the process.		
The Project Folder contains the plan, brainstorming, and tour outline documents.		

SUBTOTAL:

TOTAL POINTS (OUT OF 100):

Audio Tour: Project Map

Name _____

Subject of Tour:
(Examples: tour of school, tour of school art show, tour of Civil War battleground)

Equipment/Software to Be Used:

Audience:
(Mark all that apply)
___ Parents
___ Students (ages) _____
___ Community Members
___ Teacher and School Staff
___ People with Disabilities (list) _____
___ Other (list) _____

Distribution:
(Mark all that apply)
___ Put on Web for people to download to their own iPods or mp3 players
___ Put on iPods or mp3 players and check them out to visitors at the venue
___ Give out on CD for people to listen in their car
___ Put on CD and pass out portable CD players to visitors
___ Other (list) _____

Project Partners:

Name	E-mail	Phone	School or Community Partner?

Important Dates:

Project Assigned:	_____	Editing Completed:	_____
Conference #1:	_____	Conference to Review:	_____
Tour Outline Completed:	_____	Exporting and Distribution Due:	_____
Conference #2:	_____		
Recording Due:	_____		

Audio Tour
Brainstorming Sheet

Name _____

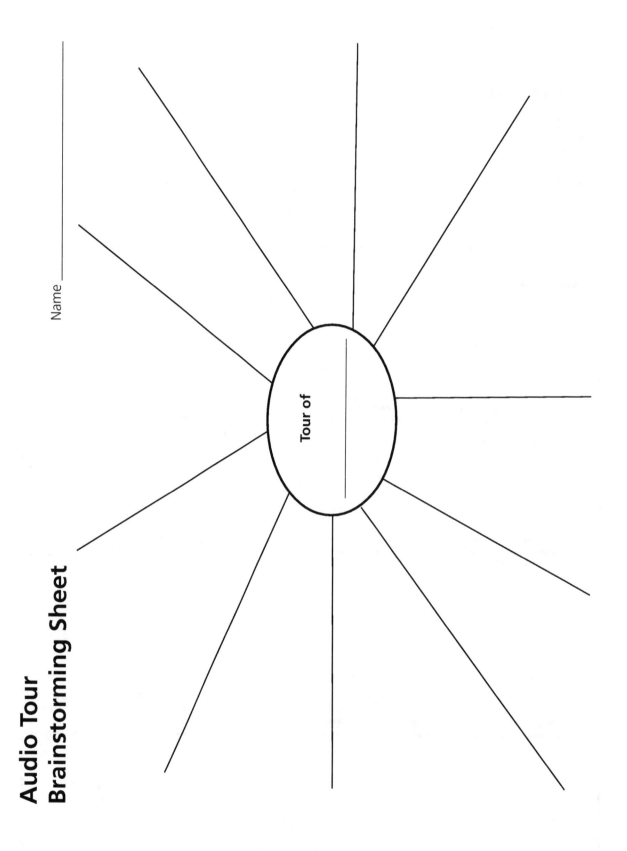

Tour of

From *Podcasting at School* by Kristin Fontichiaro. Westport, CT: Libraries Unlimited. Copyright © 2008.

On the brainstorming sheet, cross out the stops that will not be used. Next, sequence the stops by numbering them. The sequence for the tour may depend on factors such as minimizing the number of times tourists will cross the road (perhaps making sure that they always cross at a stoplight), one-way streets, and proximity of one stop to another.

The next step is to prepare a tour script. The script should begin with an *introduction,* which has the following components:

- Opening greeting

- Introduction of speakers (avoid using students' last names to protect their privacy)

- Explanation of the subject or focus of the tour

- Number of stops on the tour

- Explanation of how the listener will know that it is time to move to the next stop

- Directions to the first stop on the tour.

For each tour stop, the listener should receive the following information:

1. The name of the object or building.

2. The important information about the object. This can include the artist or architect, the year of creation, a description of the object, and its historical or cultural significance.

3. Directions to the next stop on the tour.

The tour comes to an end with a *conclusion* paragraph. The conclusion should do the following:

1. Alert the listener that the tour has reached its conclusion.

2. Thank the listener for being a part of the tour.

3. State the topic of the tour again.

4. Provide guidance about where the listener can learn more about the topic (e.g., curator's office, gift shop, title of a book, or Web site URL).

5. Tell the listener how to return the player, if applicable.

The sample scripts on pages 106 and 107 can be used to model the script elements or can be duplicated (making as many copies of the tour stop pages as needed) for use during recording. If possible, duplicate these pages onto cardstock, cut them in half, and string them together with a small ring. Cardstock is preferable to regular copy paper because it is sturdier and will move less in the speaker's hand. Regular copy paper is more flimsy, and the sound of its movement is picked up by most recorders, which is distracting.

Audio Tour: Introduction Card

Name _____

Hello. I'm (we're) _____. Welcome to this tour of _____. Our tour today has ____ stops. At each stop, you'll learn interesting information, and then you'll hear instructions for moving to the next stop on the tour.

To get started, please turn off your player and (give directions to Stop #1) _____

_____

_____. When you get there, start the recording again. Talk to you in a minute!

cut along this line

- -

Audio Tour: Conclusion Card

Name _____

We've reached the end of our tour today. Thank you for coming. I/we hope you've enjoyed getting to know more about _____. You can learn more about _____ by reading the book called _____ by _____ or by visiting this Web site (give address) _____ _____. Please return this player to _____ _____ so it can be used by another visitor.

Audio Tour:
Tour Stop #____

Name _____

In front of you, you will see *(describe the item and why it is important)*. _____

_____

_____

_____.

To move to Stop # ____, please *(give directions to next tour stop)*

_____

_____

_____.

When you get there, start the recording again.

- - - - - - - - - - - - - *cut along this line* - - - - - - - - - - - - -

Audio Tour:
Tour Stop #____

Name _____

In front of you, you will see *(describe the item and why it is important)*. _____

_____

_____.

To move to Stop # ____, please *(give directions to next tour stop)*

_____

_____

_____.

When you get there, start the recording again.

Step Three: Record It

As mentioned earlier in this chapter, portable recording equipment is ideal for this project. Because it is likely that a new file will be recorded for each stop on the tour, using a cell phone is a less ideal option, although certainly possible if it is the only equipment available. If using a cell phone with a built-in audio recording attachment, use that feature rather than sending a voice mail to Gabcast (http://www.gabcast.com) or Gcast (http://www.gcast.com). It will be easier to download the files from the phone for editing than to download them from Gabcast or Gcast's server. Be sure to have a freshly charged recorder or extra batteries to ensure success.

Choose a mild day for recording. Many recorders will pick up wind or rustling trees as static, which can make it more difficult to understand the speaker. Raindrops or thunder can also distract from the recording.

Remember that a successful audio tour can include sounds as well as narration. Consider gathering sounds as part of the tour to create a soundscape. If tourists will have to cross a busy street, remind them of traffic with a brief audio clip of cars passing. (It is also a good suggestion to ask them to take off their headphones or earbuds while crossing any street, to obey any traffic signals, and to look both ways before crossing.) If they should listen for a particular bird call while standing under the state's oldest tree, record that sound for them so they know what to be listening for. To help visitors understand the ebb and flow of Old Faithful at Yellowstone National Park, record it.

Do a few brief recording experiments to assess how far away from the speaker the recording device should be held. To minimize unwanted background noise, hold portable devices about four inches from each speaker's mouth.

If experts are available to assist with the podcast and give their permission, record their voices as well. Paid or volunteer staff often have personal connections to the locations on a tour and can share intimate stories that will make those tour stops come alive for the listener.

Especially if the tour being made is some distance from home or school, err on the side of recording too much. To facilitate editing later, make several short recordings instead of one long recording. It is easier to throw out "bad" footage when it is in small chunks than it is to locate a precise moment within a multi-minute recording.

Step Four: Edit It

Download the audio files to a computer. Use Audacity to assemble the files. Consider beginning or ending the tour with some of the soundscape sounds gathered during the tour or with music.

Step Five: Review It

Encourage students to use the rubric on page 102 to evaluate their progress to date. If possible, have students take their own tour to be sure they have not omitted any useful information. When the student and instructor agree that the project is complete, move to the distribution step.

Step Six: Distribute It

Use the instructions found in Chapter 5 to export the file into mp3 format. Upload the file to the Web so that visitors can download it and place it on their own devices, transfer it to portable mp3 players for loan to visitors, or burn it to a CD for playing in the car.

CONCLUSION

Audio tours can be a rich way to share information with others or for students to have a real-world context for acquiring, processing, and synthesizing information. The next chapter uses raps to improve students' memory and comprehension.

Chapter 11
Mnemonic Raps

■ INTRODUCTION

This chapter focuses on student-created raps. Beginning in the late 1980s, rap music became a powerful genre in the music industry. Combining a driving beat with rhythmic, often-rhyming, spoken-word text, raps were popular with students and adult listeners alike.

A *mnemonic device* is a memory-aid tool. Mnemonic raps, then, are spoken-word, rhythmic performances that contain content. In creating mnemonic raps, students gain mastery over the content. In hearing mnemonic raps, students absorb the catchy phrases, which helps them to remember important concepts and facts in preparation for higher-level thinking or assessment work.

■ POTENTIAL USES IN K–12 EDUCATION

Raps tend to be most effective when their content is on the factual recall level. Facts and other information can be distilled into short "nuggets" of content. For example, following are excerpts from potential student raps:

> **Multiplication Tables**: "Did you know about the Magic Nines? Nine times one is really fine. Nine times one always equals nine. Nine times two is a special treat. Eighteen they make, nice and neat. Nine times three equals twenty-seven. Now isn't that a number that was made in heaven?"
>
> **Procedural steps for a science experiment:** "Put your goggles on. Make sure the space is clean. Put your hands into some gloves, now you look real mean."
>
> **Steps in the writing process:** "First we think, and then outline. If you start this way, then you'll turn out fine. Then do a draft, and read it through. Give it to some friends to get their feedback, too. Then, when you know what you need to revise, do some rewrites and then check it with your eyes!"
>
> **Classroom procedures:** "When you come into our classroom, put your homework in the bin. Then look at the board and see the schedule for the day. Do the morning work, and you'll turn out OK!"

Here are some other topics for rap content:

the Periodic Table

historical events

list of presidents

the 50 states

state capitals

the planets

prepositions

continents of the world

bodies of water

branches of government

■ BEING THOUGHTFUL ABOUT LANGUAGE

Throughout the existence of the rap musical form, critics of raps have been concerned about the language used by some rappers. Swear words, derogatory comments, and streetwise slang have been common linguistic components of raps. Educators must be sensitive to the types of language they allow students to use. Following are some questions to consider before launching a rap project with students:

- **Does the school handbook cover acceptable language?** If so, remind students of the handbook language and ask that their project fall within those guidelines.

- **Do I feel comfortable having my students use streetwise language?** Some prominent rappers use slang (such as "homeboy") and nonstandard English (such as "ain't") in their raps. Especially if this is nonstandard language in your school, consider whether this language can be used in raps. For example, in a school district with a low minority enrollment, will students using this type of language accidentally mock others?

- **Are there racial, cultural, or gender-sensitive words that should be avoided?** Are there "touchstone" words that must be left out?

Being clear about language expectations up front can prevent possible glitches later.

■ PLANNING A RAP

A rap project can be successful with students in grades 5 and up in groups of as many as five students.

Before embarking on a rap project, be sure that access to rhythmic background tracks has been arranged. Audio recordings with repeating rhythmic patterns are called *loops*. Loops can be repeated over and over in a podcast to create the background rhythm pattern for a mnemonic rap. Loops and rap tracks can be found in several places. One good source of premade rap tracks for elementary school students is *Primary Rap Builder,* a CD available from Plank Road Publishing (http://www.musick8.com). Use the permissions page of the Web site to request permission to rip the CD contents to the computer for use with podcasting software and to publish the finished projects. The CD retails for approximately $30. One of its benefits is that the CD has two types of raps: some that have the background beats only, and some that are educational raps that have been made using those backgrounds, which is useful for modeling for students. The CD is geared toward the educational market.

If using Apple's GarageBand software for Mac, students can select from a variety of rhythm loops (called Apple Loops) built into the program to create a track. Once the rhythm track is created, it can be repeated again and again throughout the duration of the song.

Users of Sony Acid Music Studio products (http://www.sonycreativesoftware.com/products/acidfamily.asp) can access premade loops or buy Sony Sound Series collections of loops.

Another option is to visit magnatune.com or the social Web bookmarking service Delicious (http://del.icio.us) and search for the tag "loops" for access to loops available online. Remember that there are a variety of levels of permissions for use of loops. Be sure that the loops you select for download can be used without charge or royalty fee, either via a Creative Commons license or via other explicit permission on the host site. Be aware that *royalty-free loops* simply means that performance payments (royalties) are not required; there may still be a fee if the loop is used.

Finally, consult with a music specialist. It may be possible for students to record their own rhythm track using percussion instruments or synthesizers.

Step One: Picture It

It can be useful to begin the project by playing some sample educational raps for the class. This will help students visualize the final product.

Discuss the concepts of *verse* and *chorus* with students. A *verse* is a stanza of a song, often between four and eight lines in length. A rap can have many verses, and the content of each verse is unique. A *chorus* is a refrain or repeating series of words that comes between the verses. Each time the chorus is heard, the melody and text remain exactly the same.

Outline the topic and requirements for the assignment. Distributing a rubric at the start of the assignment can help guide the visioning process. A sample is available on page 114. Discuss the minimum time length of the podcast. For students in grades 5–8, a rap of one or two minutes is plenty. High schoolers may plan a more extensive rap.

Name _____

Rap
Evaluation Rubric

For each section, 1-10 points will be given. 10 is the highest possible score. The student will self-evaluate. The instructor will also evaluate the project and assign the final grade.

	STUDENT SCORE (1-10)	INSTRUCTOR SCORE (1-10)
CONTENT OF RAP		
The rap has a rhythmic background track.		
The rap contains at least ten accurate facts about the topic.		
The rapping is in sync with the beat of the rap track.		

RECORDING AND DISTRIBUTION SKILLS

The student navigated the podcasting software successfully.		
The document was successfully saved and exported to mp3 format.		

SPEAKING SKILLS

The words are spoken clearly and are easy to understand.		
The podcast is performed with energy and enthusiasm.		
The podcast is easy to hear when played back.		

WORK SKILLS

Deadlines were met on time, and time was used wisely.		
The student worked well with and contributed fairly to the team process.		

SUBTOTAL:		
TOTAL POINTS (OUT OF 100):		

COMMENTS

Step Two: Plan It

Work with students to devise a plan for the completion of the project. A possible outline of steps follows:

1. **Select or design an audio track.** If students are selecting a track from the Primary Rap Builder, limit the selection time to no more than 10 minutes. If students are designing an audio track, try to limit the time spent assembling loops or designing an audio track to no more than one class session. If partnering with the music specialist, who will record student-made percussion as the background track, more time may be needed.

2. **Research the topic and identify key words and ideas that are needed in the rap.** Use the brainstorming sheet on page 116 to collect these key pieces of information.

3. **Begin organizing information by topic.** Cluster related information so that the chorus and each individual verse have a unique main idea. Highlighting the brainstorming sheet using a different highlighter color for each theme or cutting apart the brainstorming sheet to cluster related ideas may be useful.

4. **Write the chorus.** The most important concept belongs in the chorus, so that it is heard repeatedly. A chorus is typically four to six lines long. An every-other-line rhyming pattern such as A-B-C-B or A-B-C-B-D-B may be employed. Another useful rhyming pattern could be A-A-B-B-C-C. Help students identify the rhythm pattern in their selected track or loop: Is it composed of four beats per line? Eight beats?

5. **Write the verses.** Now that the most key ideas have been placed in the chorus, look back at the clustered information. Create one verse for each cluster. A verse is typically four to eight lines long. The rhyming patterns described above are also suitable here.

6. **Prepare the final text.** Typing the text into the computer makes it easy to print copies for everyone. Use at least an 18-point font. If the rap takes up more than one page, consider placing the text in two columns so it fits on a single page or numbering the pages for clarity. Do not staple the pages, as the rustling paper will be picked up by the microphone.

7. **Assign parts.** It is easiest to understand what students are reciting when they do not all speak at the same time. Encourage students to break up the lines so that only one or two students will speak at once. Each student should have a part, even if one student also plays the role of the sound engineer.

8. **Warm up the voice.** Use exercises from Chapter 4.

9. **Practice the rap.** Students should play back the audio track several times and rehearse it without recording. This will develop confidence in their performance abilities, stronger knowledge of what should be chanted, and a smoother presentation.

Rap
Brainstorming Sheet

Name

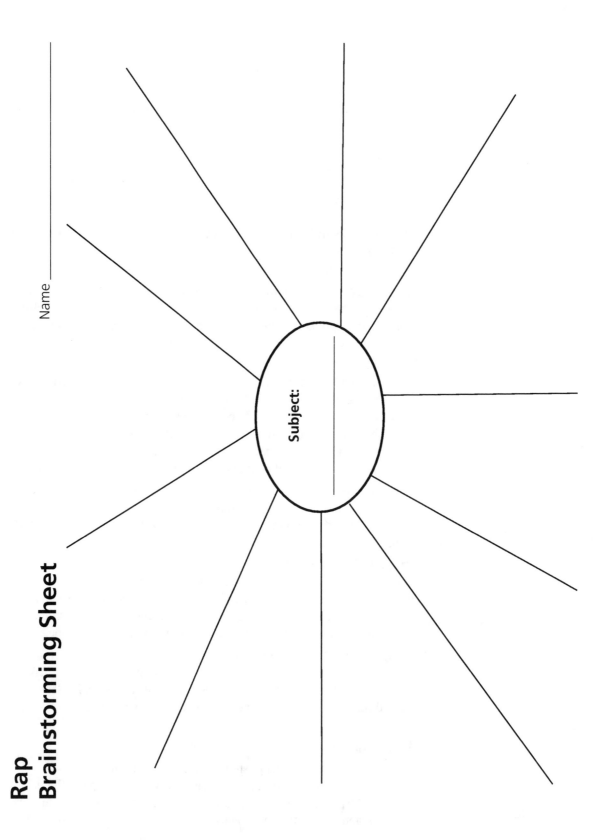

Subject:

Step Three: Record It

For this project, it is best to use a laptop or desktop with plenty of headsets daisy-chained together. Just as rock stars wear special "monitors" in their ears so they can keep time with the band, the headset narrows the slight delay between students hearing the beat and speaking to it. Avoid using a TuneTalk, Snowball, or USB microphone.

One child should act as the sound engineer, starting and stopping the recording. It may be useful to do a test recording to make sure all students' voices are approximately the same volume. The simplest way to adjust this is to ask each student to make a louder/softer sound or to adjust the distance between his or her mouth and the microphone.

If there is tremendous disparity between students' volumes, each student can be recorded individually, laying down a new track for each child on top of the previously recorded ones. Once each student's voice has been recorded, adjust the volume of each track until balance is achieved. (In Audacity, adjust the "-/+" slider to the left of the track.) However, this is a very time-consuming approach that may not be practical given classroom time constraints.

Step Four: Edit It

The primary goals for editing a mnemonic rap are the following:

- **Remove extra background music from the end of the rap**. If using Audacity, leave three seconds' worth of rhythm track after the conclusion of the vocal line, then select the Selection Tool from the top left corner, highlight any remaining "leftover" track, select EDIT > CUT, and delete the "leftover."

- **Fade out the rap track when the vocal line ends to avoid an abrupt ending.** In Audacity, highlight the last three seconds, then select EFFECT > FADE OUT from the toolbar menu.

- **Balance the volume of the vocal line.** Though manual techniques were used during the recording session to try to adjust the volume, more adjustment may be required. Using Audacity, highlight the section of sound waves that need to be louder and select EFFECT > AMPLIFY from the toolbar. Experiment with inputting different amplification numbers until you reach a balance between better volume and a slight increase in background "hiss."

- **Balance the music line with the vocal track.** Use the "-/+" slider to adjust the volume of an individual track.

When these steps have been completed, move to the reviewing stage.

Step Five: Review It

During the reviewing stage, students play back the edited podcast and use the assignment rubric to check their work against the requirements of the assignment and, as their podcasting expertise grows, against their personal barometer of a successful recording. Use the rubric on page 114.

Step Six: Distribute It

The preferred distribution method will depend on the type of background rhythm track chosen for the project and the publication and duplication rights you have been given. If you have been granted permission to use a rap track in school but not to publish it online, consider broadcasting a track each day during morning announcements. If using loops under a Creative Commons license, you will likely have the option of publishing CDs or posting the works online. Before making a decision, read the permissions section of a CD or Web site carefully.

A physical education teacher, who used mnemonic raps with her fifth-grade students to explore the "Food Pyramid," burned her students' work to a CD and played it while students moved between activity centers a few weeks later.

Another option is to burn a CD for each student. This is a positive public relations gesture, and many students, especially younger ones, like the real-world result, that they are actually creating a CD, not just a school project. Consider buying blank white CD labels and case inserts and inviting students to design a personalized album cover and CD art.

Finally, these projects can be hosted online.

■ CONCLUSION

Mnemonic raps give student creators a chance to explore content through specific rhythmic choices and give student listeners a study guide to help facilitate memorization of necessary facts. The next chapter explores how to create a variety of great radio broadcasts.

Chapter 12
Radio Broadcasts

■ INTRODUCTION

Podcasting a radio news show is a great way to share podcasting technology with the entire school. In the past, many schools lacked equipment, resources, or a radio signal for creating and sharing quality broadcasts. A podcasted radio broadcast removes these barriers and makes broadcast journalism available to all students. Students can prepare and package a broadcast, then burn it to an audio CD to be played on the school's public address system. Following that broadcast, the podcast can be archived on the school's Web page or blog.

For the purposes of this chapter, a radio broadcast podcast will be modeled on a radio magazine show. A *magazine show* is a radio show that contains a variety of segments, often strung together and introduced by a host or pair of hosts. A typical program might feature, at the beginning, an opening musical theme, a welcome from the host, and an overview of the topics to be covered in that week's broadcast. It might close with concluding thoughts from the host, perhaps reflecting on the topics of that week's broadcast or giving a *teaser* that hints at the exciting stories to be featured the following week. In the middle of the broadcast can be found a variety of potential segments:

in-studio interviews;

on-the-scene interviews;

reports about current events and interesting happenings;

reviews of books, music, movies, games, Web sites, or multimedia;

editorials;

trivia questions;

call-in advice;

advertisements (see Chapter 9);

weather forecasts;

sports updates; or

road traffic and construction updates.

The quantity and composition of interior elements of a radio magazine show will depend on the curricular connections being made, the age and abilities of the student broadcasters, and the amount of time available for the process.

■ POTENTIAL USES IN K–12 EDUCATION

Current Events Podcasts

Many of the pioneering uses of podcasting in the school setting were radio broadcasts. Some of the best-known K–12 broadcasts include Radio WillowWeb (http://www.mpsomaha.org/willow/radio), Downs FM from the United Kingdom. (http://www.downsfm.com), and Coolee Web (http://www.sdlax.net/longfellow/sc/ck/index.htm). These broadcasts use the magazine format discussed above, featuring interviews, trivia, curriculum-related stories, and more. Most of these projects used Apple's GarageBand, whose on-screen graphical interface is particularly well-suited to assembling multiple tracks and segments into a cohesive final product. These podcasts are turned into "feeds," in which behind-the-scenes code communicates with a program like iTunes. Listeners can visit iTunes, find the podcast, and subscribe to it for free. iTunes checks the radio broadcast's feed daily, so the next time the user opens his or her iTunes, the new episode is delivered.

When initiating a radio broadcast, there can be an expectation among parents and students for a radio broadcast to be repeated on a regular basis, usually weekly. A realistic sense of what can be accomplished, week in and week out, can help ensure the success of the project. Especially while getting the broadcast started, pare down the vision for a radio broadcast to no more than three elements for elementary and middle school students and no more than five for high schoolers. Once a broadcast schedule has been established, students have become comfortable with the technology and the process, and students can develop a broadcast with little teacher intervention, the broadcast can grow in length or complexity.

Alternative Radio Broadcasts: Thinking Outside the Box

The traditional radio magazine formats have been used primarily to communicate current events and perspectives to a community of peers. However, a few modifications to this format make radio broadcasts appealing for integration of curriculum areas as well.

▶ *Traveling Back in Time*

Consider using a radio broadcast as a way of gathering and sharing cultural and historical information about a specific period in time. Imagine a historical radio broadcast created in World War II, with segments giving advice on growing Victory Gardens, advertisements promoting the donation of scrap metal, news stories "live" from the battlegrounds, patriotic editorials, historically accurate theme music, and advertisements for fashions and goods of the period. Or imagine what it would be like to have a radio broadcast set in ancient Greece, with "live" performances of Greek plays, live reports about Socrates's suicide, lute music, and an interview with Aristotle.

▶ *Bringing Literature to Life*

Radio broadcasts can also be created to tie in with literary works. For example, the Harper Lee novel *To Kill a Mockingbird* could have an interview with the reclusive Boo Radley, a report from the courthouse, an editorial on the "new" educational methods being used in Scout's class, or a cooking segment with Calpurnia. Shakespeare's *Julius Caesar* could spawn a political radio broadcast, with live footage from the Senate, pundits debating Caesar's future strength, and an interview with the Soothsayer. Readers of Natalie Babbitt's *Tuck Everlasting* could intermingle advertisements for the elixir of eternal life with travel warnings not to enter the wood, weather reports predicting the summer storm, a "lost girl" alert for Winnie, live updates as the constable catches up with the Tucks, or even an exclusive interview with the eternal toad.

■ PLANNING A RADIO BROADCAST PODCAST

Step One: Picture It

Depending on the age and abilities of the target student broadcast team, this visioning step may be done either by the instructor or collaboratively by the student team. Questions to consider at the envisioning stage include the following:

- **Is this an extracurricular project or an in-class project to explore curriculum?**

- **How often will we add a new broadcast?**

- **When will students work on preparing a new broadcast?** Before school? After school? During lunch? During class?

- **Who will coordinate the project?** Will this be in addition to current duties or in place of an existing program?

- **How much broadcast complexity can the instructor take on?** How much time can be devoted to this project?

- **How will students be chosen for participation?** Who will be involved? Will everyone get a chance (this option requires ongoing training)? Or will students audition?

- **What roles will students have?** Will they have the same role for all broadcasts? Or will they rotate roles, which requires ongoing training?

- **What ground rules regarding attendance, completion of projects, parent permission/permission slips, etc., will be needed?**

- **What extra equipment will be needed?** A portable digital voice recorder or iPod for on-the-street interviews? A Macintosh to facilitate easy editing of segments using Garage Band? Software such as Podcasting Tool Factory™ for PC?

- **Who is the intended audience?** Will the focus be parents? Community? Schoolmates?

The answers to these questions will refine the vision of the podcast. If the radio broadcast is to be an assessed project, the rubric on page 123 can serve as a guideline.

Step Two: Plan It

During the planning stages, the broadcast team "works backward" from the vision and develops a series of internal deadlines in order to complete the project. Students are empowered to brainstorm and decide on stories and features, assign job functions, reserve necessary equipment, and set timelines for completion.

One or two students are chosen to be the hosts of the show. They are responsible for crafting and performing the introduction to each segment and the conclusion (including the tickler about what is coming up next time). Vincent (2005) suggests that the hosts wait until the end to write the welcoming introductory text, which should include a *teaser,* a hint at the stories that will be featured in the broadcast.

One student is chosen to be the sound engineer and is responsible for editing together all of the sections and adding background music if desired.

Another student acts as the producer, leading the planning meetings and working in partnership with the instructor to edit and evaluate scripts and interview questions for each segment. The remaining students brainstorm stories to research.

A terrific resource for planning a radio broadcast is Tony Vincent's planning sheets for Radio WillowWeb in the Omaha Public Schools (http://learninginhand. com/podcasting/RadioWillowWeb.pdf). This document gives several curriculum-related and fun suggestions for broadcast segments, with a particular focus on segments that appeal to elementary students.

The planning sheet on page 124 can assist in quickly guiding students in making these decisions.

Name _____

Radio Broadcast
Evaluation Rubric

For each section, 1-10 points will be given. 10 is the highest possible score. The student will self-evaluate. The instructor will also evaluate the project and assign the final grade.

	STUDENT SCORE (1-10)	INSTRUCTOR SCORE (1-10)
CONTENT		
The broadcast begins and ends with the host, and there are transitions between each story.		
The segment prepared by the student was of high quality.		
The segment had interview questions or a script written in advance.		
The written work demonstrated good conventions, grammar, and spelling.		
RECORDING AND DISTRIBUTION SKILLS		
The team navigated the software with little teacher intervention.		
The team distributed the finished podcast according to the directions.		
SPEAKING SKILLS		
The student spoke cleary and was easy to understand.		
The student's work had energy and enthusiasm.		
WORK SKILLS		
The student used time wisely.		
The student worked successfully and cooperatively as part of a team.		
SUBTOTAL:		
TOTAL POINTS (OUT OF 100):		

COMMENTS

Radio Broadcast Planning Sheet
Week of _____

This week's producer _____

This week's sound engineer _____

This week's host(s) _____

Segment Number	Segment Topic	Assigned to	Interview Questions or Script Due	Equipment Needed	Recording Date
0	Welcome & Intro to Segment #1	Host(s)			
1					
2	Intro to Segment #2	Host(s)			
3	Intro to Segment #3	Host(s)			
4	Intro to Segment #4	Host(s)			
5	Intro to Segment #5	Host(s)			
	Wrap-Up and Tickler for Next Time	Host(s)			

Once roles and segments have been assigned, students move forward in planning their segments. Students contact subjects to schedule interviews, draft text, and submit their drafts for review by the producer or instructor. When the written preparations have been completed and approved, students are ready to record.

Step Three: Record It

In traditional radio broadcasts, a portion of the broadcast was made "in the studio" and another portion was recorded or broadcast live "from the field," from various locations around town or around the world. Similarly, for this digital broadcast, consider two types of equipment: a computer and portable listening equipment. A central desktop or laptop computer will function as "the studio," where the host(s)'s welcoming statements, segment introductions, and farewell(s) are recorded, and where the theme music and various "from the field" segments are mixed together. Portable recording devices, such as cell phones, an iPod with recording attachment, or a digital voice recorder, enable student reporters to go where the story is without cumbersome cords or computer equipment, whether the "location" is the school gymnasium, at a community event, or in another classroom.

If using Audacity for recording, it can be useful to record each segment separately and then cut and paste it into a master Audacity file. However, if using GarageBand, which easily identifies different segments with multicolored bars, it can be easier to make multiple segments in a single file.

Step Four: Edit It

Once all the audio segments have been recorded, they can be placed in a master editing file. At this point, the key areas for editing include the following:

- **Standardizing the volume of the various segments.** One of the signs of a good sound engineer is that the listener does not have to adjust the volume for each segment. Use the "-/+" slider on the left end of each track to adjust that track's volume.

- **Assembling the segments in the correct order.** Although a preliminary order may have been sketched out on the planning sheet, the actual order may change. If one segment seems particularly strong, place it near the end of the broadcast so it does not overshadow other segments. Similarly, if another segment lacks energy or enthusiasm, position it earlier in the broadcast.

- **Finding and adding theme music to the beginning and end of the broadcast.** This is quite easy if using Mac's GarageBand software, as many sound files—known as Apple Loops—are embedded in the program for use. With Audacity it may be necessary to search for music that is designated as allowable for use during a podcast under what is known as a Creative Commons license. Creative Commons (http://www.creativecommons. org) is one source for music that has been designated by the creators as acceptable for use without requiring royalties. Magnatune (http://www. magnatune.com) is an excellent source for songs. As a courtesy, acknowledge the artist and Web site in the closing credits.

Step Five: Review It

Radio broadcasts differ from many of the other projects in this book because they are often extracurricular projects that are not assessed. If this is the case, it may be useful to spend time brainstorming a list of criteria during the envisioning stage that students will use to evaluate the success of their project and to revisit those criteria at this point in the project.

Reviewing can also occur informally, in a discussion format, if the group is relatively small (fewer than 10 students). One useful technique is "sandwiching," in which students give their feedback by "sandwiching" a constructive criticism in between two positive statements. This method is valuable because it reassures students that much of their broadcast has been a success, which buoys their confidence and makes it easier for them to hear and process the suggestions for improvement. One strategy for sandwiching is, "I liked _____. Maybe we could work on _____. I'd definitely keep _____."

A sample "sandwiching" statement from an elementary student might be the following:

> "I really like the ad for the school carnival. Maybe we could work on adding music in between the stories. I'd definitely keep the part in the interview with the P.E. teacher when he starts to laugh."

A secondary "sandwiching" statement might be more elaborate, including more explanations for why something is strong or in need of further improvement:

> "I really like the ad for the school carnival. It's got great attitude, and it's funny when they describe the principal's dunk tank like a video game. Maybe we could work on adding music between the stories to help the listener move from the mood of one story to the mood of the next. I'd definitely keep the part of the interview with the P.E. teacher where they start to laugh because it shows that our P.E. teacher has a sense of humor, which is a side many students might not know about him."

Another meaningful method of evaluation for projects that will not be formally graded is to use the performance reflection sheet on page 127.

If the broadcast is being evaluated for a grade, students can complete the student column of the rubric found on page 123.

Performance Reflection and Feedback Sheet

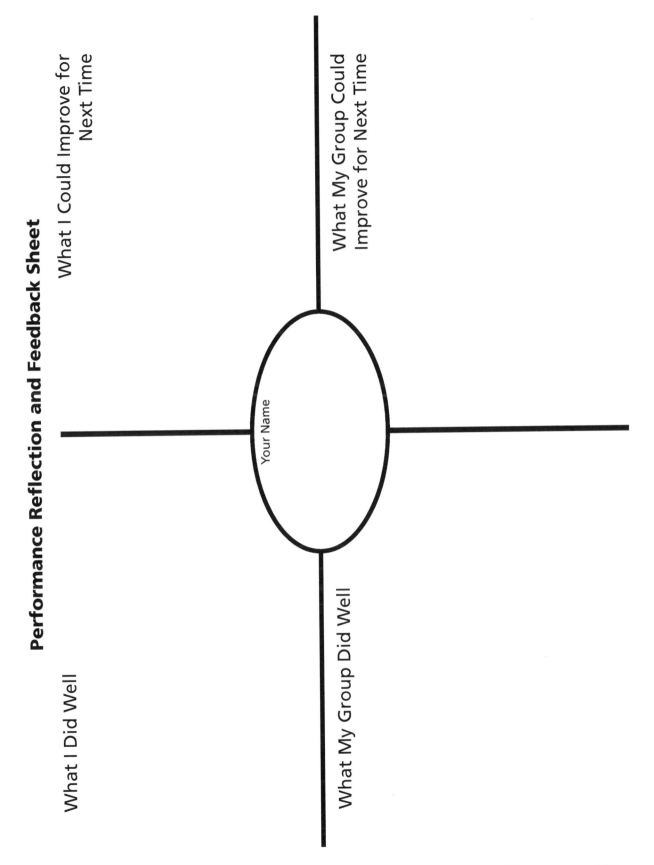

What I Could Improve for Next Time

What My Group Could Improve for Next Time

Your Name

What I Did Well

What My Group Did Well

Step Six: Distribute It

Because a radio broadcast project tends to be created as one episode in a series, consider setting up a subscription feed. A *subscription feed,* or *RSS feed,* is behind-the-scenes code that delivers your latest episode to your subscribers automatically, without the user having to visit your site. The easiest way to set this up is to create a blog dedicated just to the radio broadcasts with a link to each episode on it. The blog contains the necessary code to communicate with the user's feed-retrieval software. Refer to Chapter 6 for more information about posting podcasts to a blog. The blog will automatically generate the RSS feed that is necessary to retrieve your broadcasts.

At the time this book was written, the leading podcast-retrieval software was iTunes (http://www.apple.com/itunes), a free download for Macintosh or Windows platforms. To register your episodes with iTunes, follow the instructions at http://www.apple.com/itunes/store/podcaststechspecs.html to submit your feed for approval.

It may take a day or two for Apple to approve your feed. Once that is set, users can search the iTunes library for your podcast feed and subscribe. From then on, iTunes will check automatically for updates and deliver them to your subscribers' podcast library in iTunes.

A simpler alternative for beginning podcasters is to simply create a page on the school's Web site with a link to each podcast. One benefit of this approach is that each link can include a text summary of the episode contents. The user can quickly scan this summary and decide whether or not to click on the link to hear the episode.

■ CONCLUSION

Radio broadcasts are a popular form of podcasting. Because they fit well into the familiar format of morning announcements, but with more highly polished production values and flexible opportunities for distribution, they quickly gain the support of building administrators. Radio broadcasts are good for school environments in which working within a pattern or template is beneficial and there are adequate resources for both "studio" and "in-the-field" work.

The next chapter continues in the radio genre, this time by creating original radio plays.

Chapter 13
Radio Plays

This chapter focuses on those radio plays researched, written, and performed by students. A *radio play* is a work of theater told through voices. Radio plays were common in the pretelevision days. Serials like *The Green Hornet* and *Little Orphan Annie* kept listeners waiting expectantly for the next episode. Radio plays declined in popularity with the advent of television. However, podcasting is bringing back this once-popular format.

Radio plays rely on many of the same literary conventions as other works of fiction:

- characters who come to life through dialogue;

- written text (a script) that employs vivid, rich, descriptive language;

- a plot that features exposition, rising action, climax, falling action, and conclusion; and

- narration that moves the story along when the characters are not speaking.

Unlike written texts, radio plays also harness the power of sound to bring a world to life even more vividly. Sound effects, dramatic voices, and music heighten the mood and action of the play. Radio plays are most successful with students in grades 4 and up.

■ POTENTIAL USES IN K-12 EDUCATION

Radio plays can be incorporated into the curriculum in many ways.

- **Genre studies.** Students studying a particular literary genre (e.g., mystery or science fiction) create a radio play using the characteristics specific to that genre.

- **Re-creation of a historical event.** Students select a specific event from a history unit and create a reenactment of that event, featuring the real people, setting, and situation. For example, students might re-create Washington crossing the Delaware or the signing of the Declaration of Independence.

- **Re-creation of a scene from literature.** Students, with the guidance of the instructor, select a particular scene from a work of literature to re-create as a radio play format.

  (Note: Adapting a copyrighted work of literature is the privilege of the copyright holder. Copyright's fair use clause may be valid if your podcast will be heard or distributed only inside the classroom in which it was made. Before publishing to the Web, request permission from the copyright holder; many will gladly grant permission.)

- **Re-creation of a scene from a dramatic play.** Perhaps the simplest adaptation of all is to use a script that has already been written! Add character voices, music, and sound effects, and this can be an easy way to breathe life into an English curriculum. For example, an English teacher working on Shakespeare's *Romeo and Juliet* with four classes could, by dividing those four classes up into several groups of three to five students, create enough groups for each to record a scene of the play. As the students explore the text in-depth to prepare it for a performance, they dig more deeply into the meaning of the words, and because each group has responsibility for only a single scene, the project can be completed quickly, with just a day or two of planning in the classroom and a single visit to the computer lab to record. Music and sound effects can bring the scenes to life. When all of the groups' projects are completed, the scenes are assembled into chronological order and burned to a CD. The students' work becomes an audio study guide for the end-of-unit assessment. Future students, especially those with learning disabilities or comprehension difficulties, can use the CD as a means of understanding the text when the play is read the following year. Due to the sophistication of most plays, this technique is recommended for high school students.

- **Historical fiction.** Perhaps the most challenging and rewarding type of radio play project is to study a particular era in history and create a fictional work set in that period. In Bloom's Taxonomy of thinking, synthesis represents the highest level of thinking, because in that stage, students take existing knowledge and transform it into a new, creative product (Krathwohl 2002). A historical fiction radio play asks students to gather historical research and create original story elements based on the events, behaviors, mores, beliefs, fashions, goods, and actions of that period. Historical fiction radio plays are also appealing to teachers because they are so unique, they are almost impossible to plagiarize. Historical fiction radio plays are recommended for students in grades 5 and up.

The following steps for creating a radio play are based on a historical fiction radio play.* To create one of the other types mentioned earlier, simply remove the unnecessary steps from the following sequence.

For a historical fiction radio play podcast, consider devoting to it two or three sessions a week for three weeks. In week one, envision the project, research, and plan it. In week two, synthesize the research and write the script. In week three, brainstorm sound effects and record, edit, and publish the podcast.

*Note: An earlier version of this project appeared in the author's *Active Learning Through Drama, Podcasting, and Puppetry* (Libraries Unlimited, 2007).

Step One: Picture It

▶ *Introducing the Format*

Because today's students are unfamiliar with radio plays of the past, it can be useful to introduce radio plays to them by playing some examples. To hear some examples of historical fiction radio plays made by fifth-grade students, visit http://beverlymedia.edublogs.org/2007/05/29/5th-grade-western-expansion-projects-here/.

▶ *Selecting a Topic*

Students, working in groups of three to five, then select a topic within the curriculum area of study. For example, if the class is studying the Civil War, a group might choose Lincoln's Gettysburg Address, the surrender at Appomattox, or the Buffalo Soldiers. For younger students, the instructor may wish to generate a list of preapproved topics from which the students may choose.

▶ *Knowing the Expectations*

Distributing the project rubric at the beginning of the project helps students know what is expected of them. The rubric on page 132 does not focus solely on the final product. It also evaluates the research process, the group's work habits, the script, and the performance.

Step Two: Plan It

▶ *Planning Sheet*

In addition, students receive a planning sheet (see page 133), which is a one-page summary of the project that includes space for initial research questions, items needed from home, and deadlines. If possible, assign each student a folder in which to store all project materials.

Students use the planning sheet to record initial thoughts as they explore their topic. As students research, taking notes or highlighting computer printouts, they record early research questions and thoughts for their play.

▶ *Initial Research Conference*

Planning a group conference with the instructor after the first research session can help make sure the research questions are valid, begin to examine the possible dramatic structure and content of the script, and assess for any inaccuracies or deficiencies in understanding.

If a classroom teacher is partnering with a media specialist on this project, consider dividing the class in half, with half the class having the teacher as a "coach" and the other half having the media specialist as a "coach."

Radio Play
Evaluation Rubric

For each section, 1-5 points will be given; 5 points is the highest. The student will self-evaluate. The instructor will also evaluate the project and assign the final grade.

RESEARCH

	STUDENT SCORE (1-5)	INSTRUCTOR SCORE (1-5)
Research began by reading an encyclopedia entry.		
I wrote at least two preliminary questions for our first planning conference.		
I participated in planning conferences with my team and instructors.		
We created plans at the conferences.		
My team used at lesat three online sources for research and printed them out.		
The sources we used were of high quality.		
I highlighted and took notes on my Web printouts.		

TEAMING

I worked well as a member of a team.		
Work was shared equally by all teammates.		

PROJECT

Our script is historical fiction.		
Our script contains accurate facts and historical information.		
Our script has a logical sequence of events.		
Our script has good spelling, punctuation, and capitalization.		
Our script is neatly typed.		
Our bibliography is complete, neat, and typed.		

PRESENTATION

We began our recording with the title and our first names (no last names).		
We successfully recorded our play and exported it to mp3 format.		
Our play includes original and creative sound effects.		
Our play is presented with enthusiasm.		
Voices are interesting and have variety and inflection.		

SUBTOTAL:	
TOTAL POINTS (OUT OF 100):	

Planning Sheet:
Radio Play

Name _____

Other Students in Group: _____

_____

Initial Research Questions (What do we need to find out first in our research?)

Roles in Our Play:

Role   Played by

_____ _____

_____ _____

_____ _____

_____ _____

_____ _____

_____ _____

--continue on back side of paper if needed--

We will need these sound effects:

Item   Will be brought/made by:

_____ _____

_____ _____

_____ _____

_____ _____

_____ _____

_____ _____

--continue on back side of paper if needed--

Important Dates:

Project Assigned: _____   Class Rehearsals: _____
Conference #1:   _____   Recording Date: _____
In-Class Research Dates: _____   Folder & Rubric Due: _____
Script due: _____
Conference #2:   _____

▶ *Self-Evaluation*

At the conclusion of the first week, the research should be completed. Especially if working with a large group of students, a student self-evaluation at this point is useful to the instructor. The student self-evaluation shown on page XX is structured as a letter to encourage students to see the instructor as a partner and an ally in the project. The questions in the student self-evaluation probe into several areas, giving the instructor a well-rounded view of the student's perception of the project.

▶ *Writing the Script*

In the second week the project shifts to writing the script. A *script* is a document containing the words spoken by performers in a play. Radio play scripts also include sound effects.

If possible, use a word processing program instead of a handwritten script. The text will be easier to read, it is easy to make duplicate copies, and fresh copies can be printed after each round of revisions.

Divide the page into two columns. In the narrow left column, write the name of the character (or, if the plot is being moved forward at points by the use of a narrator, use the word "Narrator"). In the wider right column, the spoken text appears. If a sound effect is needed, it is denoted by the abbreviation "SFX" in the left column, and a description of the sound effect is placed in the right column. (The "S" stands for "sound," and "FX" is a phonetic spelling shorthand for "effects.") The sample on page 136 shows how a formatted script might appear.

When students have finished writing the script, they are ready to experiment with sound effects and music.

Radio Play Self-Evaluation, End of Week 1

Over the past several days, you have researched using a variety of sources. Before your group begins outlining the script, take a moment to reflect on your progress in this letter to your instructor coach.

Dear Coach _____,

Here is how I feel about the research I have collected:

_____

_____

_____.

We think our historical fiction plot might be about this:

_____

_____

_____.

I am doing well with:

_____

_____

_____.

I don't understand or am worried about:

_____

_____

_____.

I also want you to know that:

_____

_____

_____.

Signed, _____

The Road to the West
A radio play by Julie, Quinton, Quincy, and Grace

SFX:	Intro music -- cowboy style (from Magnatune.com). Lower volume when Narrator begins to speak.
Narrator:	Welcome to **The Road to the West**, a radio play by Julie, Quinton, Quincy, and Grace. In this play, Quinton plays a guide on the road and the homesteader Mr. Smith. Grace plays his wife, Mrs. Smith, Quincy plays their son George, and Julie is the narrator.
SFX:	Music fades away.
Mrs. Smith:	Good morning, husband. It is a beautiful, sunny day.
Mr. Smith:	Not nice enough, I'm afraid. I just can't make enough money here on our farm to keep us going from year to year.
George:	Hey, Pa! Look what's in this newspaper! It says, "Go West, Young Man!" What if we traveled out West? There's plenty of land there, just waiting to be claimed by families like us!
Mrs. Smith:	I don't know, Pa. We might be lonely out in the West all by ourselves, without our family and friends nearby.
Narrator:	The Smith family decided to give themselves one month to think about going West. It was a terrible month. The rains came and flooded their fields.
SFX:	Rain.
Narrator:	And then the winds came and blew their seeds away.
SFX:	Wind.
Narrator:	By the time a month was up, they had agreed to pack up and go West.

Sound Effects

A *sound effect* is a nonspoken sound. Sound effects are still an important part of telling stories in the entertainment world. Foley artists add sound effects to movies. Watch for "Foley artist" in the credits of a film.

Sound effects can serve two purposes. First, they can help create a sense of atmosphere (such as thunder, rain, or the cheers of a crowd), and second, they can help the listener visualize the actions of the play (such as the sound of horses' hooves, a cork being popped out of a bottle of champagne, or a slammed door).

There are many sources for sound effects. Sound CDs can be purchased, ripped to the computer, and imported into Audacity. GarageBand, Tool Factory Podcasting, and other more sophisticated programs have sound libraries built into the software. Sound effects are available from some Web sites free of charge and from others for a small fee. For an excellent selection of sound effects, try A1 Sound Effects (http://www.a1freesoundeffects.com/radio.html). If time permits, the most creative challenge for students is to create their own sound effects. Listeners of Garrison Keillor's public radio program *A Prairie Home Companion* may know that Keillor's show is one of the last to use a "sound effects man," who manipulates simple objects to create sound effects from scratch. You can hear vintage episodes of *A Prairie Home Companion* and share those sound effects with students by visiting http://www.prairiehome.org.

Students can create a waterfall by pouring water from a bottle into a dish pan. They can make the wind rustle by shaking loose papers over the microphone. They can take off their shoes and tap them on the table to sound like walking. They can record a ticking clock to develop suspense, the hum of the trash compactor for a science fiction piece, or the "beep" of the media center's circulation desk wand for a ticking time bomb.

Ask the music specialist(s) in the building to lend you small rhythm instruments. Cymbals, small drums, maracas, rain sticks, and other nonmelodic instruments can create intriguing effects when recorded.

Gunshots are featured in many radio plays. Due to school safety concerns, do not encourage students to create this effect, as even a false gunshot is alarming in a school setting. The Web site A1 Sound Effects (http://www.a1freesoundeffects. com/radio.html) has a selection of gunshot sounds that can be downloaded for use. If other jarring sound effects such as screaming will be recorded, place a sign outside the classroom door so that passersby do not become concerned.

As the script develops and sound effects are chosen, give each group a labeled dish pan, tote bag, or box in which to store their sound effects. (Do not use a crate, as small items can fall through the holes.) Encourage students to bring in sound effects objects far in advance of the performance week to make sure that they will not be forgotten at the last minute.

Making a master list of sound effects on the planning sheet helps students take a quick inventory of what they have and what is needed.

▶ *Second Conference*

The second conference is held at the conclusion of the second week, after the script has been drafted. The instructor proofreads the script, checking for historical accuracy, characterization, pacing, and plot development. In addition, students talk with the instructor about their plans for preparing for performance, including the sound effect objects they will create and the changes in vocal pitch, volume, speed, and energy that will set each character apart.

One student is chosen to be the sound engineer. He or she is responsible for running the computer, starting and stopping during recording, and playing back the recorded podcast for his or her classmates. This prevents squabbles among the group members. The sound engineer may also speak additional roles during the radio play.

▶ *Rehearsal*

Week three begins with rehearsal and ends with performance. The purpose of the rehearsal is to familiarize students with the flow and text of the script and to practice with sound effects. Review some of the warm-up exercises from Chapter 4 with students beginning at the rehearsal stage.

Students may wish to record several of their rehearsals, play them back, and discuss areas for improvement. The performance reflection sheet on page 127 can help to facilitate this process in advance of the "final" recording period, as can the "sandwiching" technique discussed on page 126. If, during the rehearsal process, it is discovered that more information is needed, permit students to return to the research phase, add sound effects, or make changes. This models the way in which adults process information in the real world.

Step Four: Record It

As novice performers, students sometimes speed through their text in a monotone if asked to rehearse for too long. When students are able to move easily through their text and sound effects, it is time to stop rehearsing and begin recording.

Place a copy of the instruction sheet from page 37 next to each computer. Place one copy of the script on the keyboard, and have the sound engineer sit at the computer. If the school has an extra room, such as a conference room or empty office, set up a recording station there to minimize background noise. If this is not possible, give the rest of the class a quiet task, such as silent reading, while a group records.

Step Four: Edit It

For some students recording and editing will intermingle, as they may choose to re-record something on the spot, rather than waiting until the editing stage. This is fine. Others will begin to edit out extraneous pauses once the content has been recorded. Using the options in Audacity's Effects menu, students can boost the sound of weak areas of the recording (EFFECT > AMPLIFY), fade out music or sound effects (EFFECT > FADE OUT), add an echo (EFFECT > ECHO), and more. Some may discover that more text is needed or that adding a pause would be useful (GENERATE > SILENCE).

Some will discover that adding music underneath the entire podcast may help animate the story and propel it forward. The music at Magnatune (http://www. magnatune.com) can be searched by genre. Follow the site's onscreen instructions for downloading and using Magnatune recordings in podcasts at no cost.

Step Five: Review It

In a project of this duration, reviewing and self-reflection are embedded into each step of the process. At this point in the project, students should complete the "student" column of the scoring rubric. Weak areas may be corrected. If they find that the podcast meets their personal goals for quality as well as the requirements for the assignment, they have completed the project and may turn in their project folder for formal assessment by the instructor.

Step Six: Distribute It

Radio plays may be shared in many ways. Save them to the desktop and host a listening day. Alternatively, put a different play on each media center computer; set up headphones; and invite students' family members, colleagues, and faculty to visit the listening kiosks. Need an interactive activity near the media center during parent–teacher conferences or curriculum night, when the Book Fair obscures the normal activities of the media center? Set up the listening kiosks in the hallway (check with the custodian to be sure that is compatible with fire exit regulations).

Parents also enjoy having these projects online. Send home an invitation inviting families to your blog, where they can click to hear the radio plays and leave a comment for students. Parents like to send the link on to out-of-town relatives. Request that the link to the projects be placed in the informational packets for the board of education or included in district flyers home.

■ CONCLUSION

Though radio plays take time, they are wonderful opportunities for higher-level thinking and creativity. Students are motivated to research deeply, process information, and share it in this creative format.

The next chapter takes podcasting to a personal level via oral history interviews.

Chapter 14
Oral History Projects

▆ INTRODUCTION

Technology is most rewarding when it draws people closer together. Using podcasting equipment to capture oral history interviews can be one of the most touching, meaningful uses for a podcast. When we invite people to recall and share memories in their authentic voices, we gain their perspectives on the world. For students, oral interviews make history real. Textbook events come alive when viewed through personal experience. Events become intimate, and the abstract becomes personal.

There are several existing oral history projects. They can pave the way for a successful oral history project of your own. One of the best known oral history project is the Fortunoff Video Archive for Holocaust Testimonies of Yale University Library (http://www.library.yale.edu/testimonies/), which used video to capture the testimony of Holocaust survivors. The Veterans History Project, a project of the American Folklife Center of the Library of Congress (http://www.loc.gov/vets/), invites amateurs and professionals to interview veterans to gather high-quality audio interviews with civilians and veterans affiliated with the military conflicts since World War I. The StoryCorps project (http://www.storycorps.net) travels the United States, providing a sound engineer and professional-quality equipment for family oral history interviews. Participants receive a CD as a personal memento of the experience, and selected interviews are broadcast on National Public Radio.

▆ POTENTIAL USES IN K–12 EDUCATION

Oral history projects are a powerful way to connect students to the past, to community members, and to their families. This chapter explores two models for an oral history project. The first is a classroom model, in which students work under the guidance of an instructor to interview family or community members according to a particular theme. The second model is an oral history station at a school event such as parent–teacher conferences or open house. These stations encourage parents and students to take a break from the hustle and bustle of school life to converse with one another. Using interview questions suggested by the school staff or decided at the family level, family interviews connect generations and provide a moment of intimacy that is captured forever.

■ PLANNING A CLASSROOM-BASED ORAL HISTORY PROJECT

Oral history projects document the life and perspectives of the interviewee, provide practice and insight for the interviewer, and inform the listener.

Classroom-based oral history projects have a curriculum or thematic connection. Oral histories work extremely well with history or social studies, where students sometimes struggle to understand the impact of historical events on the daily lives of those in their community. These interviews often begin with the cliché, "Where were you on the night that _____?" Possible areas for interviews include the following:

World War II: life at home in the United States or life as a soldier

Korean War

Assassination of Martin Luther King Jr.

Assassination of John F. Kennedy or Robert Kennedy

Sputnik

First U.S. flight into space

Vietnam War

Explosion of the space shuttle *Challenger*

First time the person went online

Wars in Iraq and Afghanistan

Local history events

Oral history projects can also be successful in secondary journalism classes, where students are learning to conduct a strong interview. At all points on the K–12 continuum, instructional units that focus on families or identity also benefit from oral history projects.

Oral history projects don't just record memories from the past. They can also capture the thoughts, beliefs, and emotions of the present for posterity. Think of how capturing people's reactions on September 11, 2001, a day of great fear and confusion, would benefit future scholars. How could an enterprising class oral history project capture the thoughts and feelings of new military recruits about to ship out to Iraq? People who have just become citizens of the United States? Local athletes about to depart for the next Olympic Games, World Series, Super Bowl, or Paralympics?

On a more personal level, oral history interviews can capture important social moments in a student's life. Consider capturing oral history interviews at the Senior All-Night Party and burning them to a CD as a memory of high school. At religious schools, interview students on the eve of important religious landmarks: their bar or bat mitzvah, confirmation, or first communion. Interview a teen on the eve of her *quinceañera*, a special party in Hispanic cultures that honors a teenage girl's fifteenth birthday. Fifth- or eighth-grade graduation, National Honor Society inductions, and sports banquets are wonderful backdrops for oral history interviews. Is an old school being torn down? Gather memories in podcast form and put them in a time capsule in the foundation of the new building.

Step One: Picture It

In most classroom oral history projects, the instructor establishes the overall theme and may even preselect the people who will be interviewed. Therefore, during the picturing stage, the instructor's goal is to explain the goal of the project, the curricular connection, and how students will prepare for and interact with the interviewee.

Sharing the evaluation rubric can help students visualize the process and the product (page 144). The instructor also builds excitement for the project, how the project will be shared with others, and the unique opportunity that oral history work presents.

Play a few sample oral history interviews from StoryCorps (http://www.storycorps.net) or read a few interviews from the book about StoryCorps, *Listening Is an Act of Love* (Isay 2007), to help students visualize the interview experience. Point out that part of what makes an oral history interview memorable is that people speak authentically and naturally. Unlike a job interview, where a certain formality shapes the discussion, oral history interviews flourish when people speak as themselves.

Step Two: Plan It

During the planning stage, students plan, schedule, and prepare for a successful interview.

▶ Select an Interviewee

First, select a community member to be the *interviewee* (the person being interviewed). Sometimes teachers select the pool of interviewees in advance before beginning the assignment in order to ensure that the project is viable. In other situations, the students may use local community resources to find someone to interview. For war memorial projects, contact local veterans' organizations such as the Veterans of Foreign Wars (http://www.vfw.org) or American Legion (http://www.legion.org). A local synagogue can help connect students with survivors of the Holocaust. A senior citizen activity center can connect the vibrant memories of its members with the enthusiasm of your students. For impromptu interviews, ask the local public library for permission to create a small recording area in a quiet corner of the lobby and invite patrons to stop by and comment on the selected topic. If the local shopping mall has a quiet area for relaxing and sitting, perhaps they will allot some space for the project as well.

If recording veterans' interviews for the Library of Congress's Veterans History Project, be sure to consult the resources at http://www.loc.gov/vets at the beginning of the planning stage to be sure that the project and procedures fit within their project standards.

Name _____

Oral History Project
Evaluation Rubric

For each section, 1-10 points will be given. 10 is the highest possible score. The student will self-evaluate. The instructor will also evaluate the project and assign the final grade.

		STUDENT SCORE (1-10)	INSTRUCTOR SCORE (1-10)
CONTENT			
	The project contains a complete introduction.		
	The project contains a complete conclusion.		
	The student demonstrated active listening skills.		
	The student prepared interview questions in advance.		
RECORDING AND DISTRIBUTION SKILLS			
	The student navigated the software with little teacher intervention.		
	The student distributed the finished podcast according to the directions.		
SPEAKING SKILLS			
	The student spoke clearly and was easy to understand.		
	The student had energy and demonstrated interest in the person being interviewed.		
WORK SKILLS			
	The student used planning time wisely.		
	The student made contact with the interviewee at appropriate times during the planning process.		

SUBTOTAL: ☐

TOTAL POINTS (OUT OF 100): ☐

COMMENTS

Consult with district administration about the need for an interviewee permission slip. It can be useful for the interviewee to know how the recording will be used. Sample text could be:

I agree to be interviewed and recorded by _____
on the subject of _____ as part of _____ High
School's _____ class. I understand that the final recording will be
played in class/posted to the Web/burned to CD/donated to the Library of
Congress and give permission for this distribution. I know that I will receive a CD copy of the final interview and can withdraw my participation at
any time.

Signed _____

Date _____

Telephone _____

E-mail (optional) _____

In addition, make sure that the interviewee knows how to contact the instructor via telephone or e-mail, as well as the best time to contact him or her.

▶ Planning the Questions

Next, create a list of possible interview questions. The brainstorming sheet on page 146 can help students identify areas for questioning and then sequence them.

One important thing for students to keep in mind when writing interview questions is to avoid questions that can be answered with "yes," "no," or a single word. For example, asking, "Did you like your senior prom?" is likely to get "Yes" or "No" as an answer, and the interview will stall. But if the question is tweaked into, "*What* did you like about your senior prom?" the interviewee is more likely to give a longer, more elaborate answer. Similarly, "Describe your dog" will result in a more interesting answer than, "What kind of dog was he?" for which the answer will likely be simply the name of the breed.

If "single-word questions" become necessary to the interview, plan a second *follow-up question,* a question that asks for more information. Notice how in the interview sample below, the interviewer follows up a one-word answer ("Rover") with a request for more information about the dog.

Interviewer: What was your dog's name?

Interviewee: Rover.

Interviewer: Can you describe him for us?

Interviewee: He was a golden retriever. He was very playful, and he liked to dig for bones under the maple tree in our front yard. Did I ever tell you about that maple tree? He dug there for years but never found any bones.

Oral History
Interview Brainstorming Sheet

Name _____

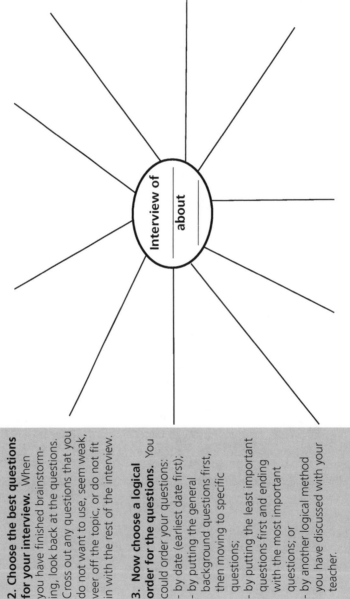

How to Use This Sheet

1. Brainstorm questions on this sheet.

2. Choose the best questions for your interview. When you have finished brainstorming, look back at the questions. Cross out any questions that you do not want to use, seem weak, veer off the topic, or do not fit in with the rest of the interview.

3. Now choose a logical order for the questions. You could order your questions:
- by date (earliest date first);
- by putting the general background questions first, then moving to specific questions;
- by putting the least important questions first and ending with the most important questions; or
- by another logical method you have discussed with your teacher.

4. Prepare your final interview outline.
- Write an introduction.
- Type your interview questions, in order, using an 18-point font.
- Write the conclusion.

Tips for Writing Great Interview Questions

1. Avoid questions that can be answered with yes or no. "Did you like traveling during the war?" will give you a one-word answer. "What did you like about traveling during the war?" will give you a much more interesting response.

2. Stay neutral. Keep focused on the thoughts and opinions of the person you are interviewing.

3. Don't be afraid to ask a follow-up question based on your previous question.

4. Ask for specific examples.

5. Start with a few comfortable questions so your interviewee doesn't feel nervous.

Interview of _____ about _____

For nonmilitary interviews, StoryCorps has a remarkable Question Generator (http://www.storycorps.net/participate/question_generator/). First it asks for some preliminary information, including names and the questioner's e-mail address. Based on the information given, the Question Generator creates a list of potential questions, customized with the interviewee's name. Check the questions that have the most appeal, and move to the next screen, where questions can be customized and placed in a meaningful order. Click the button at the bottom of the screen, and a completed list of questions is presented. Print the list of questions, and the interviewer is ready to go. Best of all, the questions are e-mailed to the interviewer, which reduces the amount of time spent typing out questions. Students can forward this e-mail to their instructor as evidence of their preparation for the interview.

If conducting a veteran interview, the Veterans History Project has a Suggested Questions for Veterans page that structures the interview into six sections:

1. For the Record (basic information about the person being interviewed)

2. Jogging Memory (questions about enlistment and boot camp)

3. Experiences (the wars in which the veteran saw active duty, job function, captivity, medals)

4. Life (personal activities and reflections)

5. After Service (life in the early time after leaving the service)

6. Later Years and Closing (reflections, other items not covered yet in the interview)

Detailed questions for each stage in the interview can be found at http://www.loc.gov/vets/vetquestions.html.

▶ Write the Introduction

Oral history interviews are essentially primary source material. Create an introduction that establishes some context. The interviewer should write a simple informative paragraph in which the interviewer identifies himself or herself (using first names only to protect student privacy), who is being interviewed, where they are, what the date is, and the general topic of the interview. For example:

> "I'm Jamal, and I'm here with my grandmother, Sadie Jones. We are at her house in Brooklyn, New York. Today is January 31, 2008. Our interview today is about her experiences during the civil rights movement."

▶ Write the Conclusion

It can be useful to prewrite the conclusion to the interview as well. First, the interviewer invites the interviewee to add any further thoughts that might not have been covered elsewhere in the interview. Including this step makes sure that the interviewee's expectations for the interview are met. Saying, "We're almost out of time. Is there anything else you'd like to add?" or, "Before we bring this interview to an end, I want to give you the chance to add anything we haven't already discussed" will suffice. After that, the interviewer states that the interview has reached its conclusion and thanks the interviewee.

Step Three: Record It

▶ *Minimize Noisy Distractions*

Both StoryCorps (http://www.storycorps.net/participate/do-it-yourself_guide/how_to_interview/) and the Veterans History Project (http://www.loc.gov/vets/moreresources.html) remind interviewers of the importance of sound quality to the final product. Rooms with a lot of soft furnishings, like living rooms full of upholstered furniture and carpeting, generally make a better recording area than rooms with many hard surfaces, such as a kitchen, where sound can bounce against the hard surfaces, creating an echo.

Before recording, remove or minimize possible distractions: buzzing fluorescent lights, noisy heating and cooling units, squeaky chairs, ticking clocks, and telephones. Remove "noisy" jewelry such as charm bracelets or dangly earrings.

If working in a school, try not to schedule a recording to occur while classes will be changing, as the increase in noise and the bells will be distracting. Borrow a staff member's office to minimize outside noise if possible.

▶ *Set up the Equipment*

The equipment being used will depend on the setting for the interview. If a quiet, carpeted office at school can be made available for the interviews, recording with headsets and a computer will probably yield the best quality, because the headsets will minimize extraneous noise. If this is not possible, another option is to daisy-chain two headset microphones into a portable recording device such as a digital voice recorder. The last choice is to use a portable recording device without an external microphone jack.

▶ *Test the Equipment*

Podcasting an oral history project is a new experience for most people, who are not used to hearing their own voices. To settle nerves (and get a sense of the quality of the sound recording), make a test recording. Have the interviewer read the introduction and ask a simple question or two. (Example: "Describe what you're wearing today.") End with the conclusion. This familiarizes the interviewee with the framework of the interview. Take a moment to play back the recording. Modify sound levels and equipment as needed.

▶ *Conduct the Interview*

While student oral history interviews should have preplanned questions as a basic structure, they are merely a starting point. The goal is to have a meaningful conversation. The key to a great interview is stay in the moment. If the interviewee, in responding to a question, brings up a topic that sounds interesting, it is OK to go "off script" and ask about it. Avoid the urge to hurry on to the next question. Keep listening, and ask new questions that come to mind. Stay in the moment, and when the moment has ended, return to the list of questions. For example, in the sample interview earlier in this chapter, the interviewee asked, "Did I ever tell you about the maple tree?" Even if the interviewer's next question was more about the dog Rover, he or she may wish to learn more about the maple tree, and so his or her next question might be, "You mentioned a maple tree in your yard, and I never saw that in any of the pictures of your house. Can you tell me more about it?" Young and inexperienced interviewers will have a more difficult time veering from the prescribed questions and following the interviewee's sideline of thought.

Encourage students to look at the person who is talking and maintain eye contact. StoryCorps recommends nodding instead of saying, "Uh huh," to demonstrate active listening. Active listening can activate new interview questions and new areas for conversation.

If there are disruptions during the interview, such as an unexpected announcement on the school's public address system, students can stop the interview for a moment, note the time of the interruption (to make it easy to find and cut out during editing), then repeat the last question so the interviewee can try again without interruption.

▶ *After the Interview*

When the recording is over, the student should thank the interviewee for participating. The interviewee should receive the following information: the name and contact information of the coordinating teacher, the projected timeline for when the final recording will be ready, and the location online of the final interview (if applicable). The interviewer should make sure that he or she has the interviewee's address so a complimentary CD can be sent. If the oral history project will culminate in a public event, such as an open house or reception, confirm that the interviewee has received an invitation.

Because it can be difficult to reschedule an oral history interview (see Step Five), the instructor (if present) might ask the student to step aside for a few moments, then replay a few moments of the recording to check for technical quality and review the project against the rubric (see page 144).

Step Four: Edit It

Editing is almost always done without the presence of the interviewee. Editing an oral history interview can be different from editing an interview for a radio broadcast (see Chapter 12). An oral history interview is a documentary project, whereas a radio broadcast interview is designed to entertain and inform. Therefore, oral history projects may be far longer (the Veterans History Project suggests a minimum of 30 minutes) and does not need to be edited down merely to fit into a time limit.

As a rule, try to keep in as much information as possible. Edit out only the major distractions, such as a coughing fit or a question that was re-answered when it was interrupted by the fire alarm the first time.

Step Five: Review It

Use the rubric for student self-evaluation. With an oral history interview, it can be difficult to reschedule or redo the interview, as might be recommended for other podcasting projects. Beyond the scheduling difficulties, it can be difficult to recapture the spontaneous, unscripted feel of the first "take."

Step Six: Distribute It

A complimentary CD should be given to the participant. In addition, if the participant agrees, the project can be uploaded to a school Web site or blog, shared with another oral history project, or donated to the Veterans History Project.

▪ Planning an Oral History Station at a School Event

While an oral history project that ties itself to the curriculum is an excellent strategy for bringing personal and political history to life, hosting an oral history station at a school event is a way of bringing families together through technology.

An oral history station, hosted either in the media center or in the hallway outside, can be a way to demonstrate the important role of the media center and its staff in integrating technology into student learning experiences. An oral history station can be coordinated by a school library media specialist, perhaps with the assistance of students or parent volunteers. Because a great number of people will cycle through the stations in a short period of time, sample questions are provided by the staff.

Step One: Picture It

Stop and think for a moment. What would this project look like if it were successful? Pairs of family members hunched intimately over the computer, talking quietly but intently to one another. Parents saying, "That was a wonderful experience; I hope you'll do that every year so we can slip the CD into our daughter's memory book." Children proudly showing off their podcasting skills to their family members. Parents recording a podcast with their children, then returning an hour or two later so the experience can be repeated with a different family member. Parents asking if it's possible to string together one more set of headphones so that both parents can talk simultaneously with the child. School staff members helping get the families oriented, then stepping away to let the families spend some much-needed quiet reflection time together, returning at the end to take care of exporting and uploading the file.

Step Two: Plan It

The first step in establishing oral history stations is to select a location for the activity. Ideally, there is a quiet room or area adjoining the media center with ample space and power outlets for two or three computer stations. If no other options are available, try placing two or three computers in the hallway. This draws more visibility to the event, although sound quality will be diminished.

Next, determine the number of staff members available to support the oral history project. Allow no more than three computer stations for each volunteer. Use a Y-adapter, as discussed in Chapter 3, to join together two headsets to the computer. Label each computer with a letter to make it easy to keep track of which recordings were made at each computer.

Finally, prepare a small brochure that describes the project, offers simple questions to answer, and gives simple tips for operating the Audacity software. Pages 151 and 152 can be duplicated into a double-sided brochure and folded in half into a small booklet.

Place posters around the school advertising the oral history stations and put notices in school or classroom newsletters. If desired, add a link to the StoryCorps Question Generator (http://www.storycorps.net/participate/question_generator/) for families who would like to create their own interview questions.

Welcome to the Family Oral History Project!

What Is It?
The Family Oral History Project is a chance for families to share memories with each other and to preserve those memories online or on a CD.

It's easy!
1. Take a moment to reflect together on the questions on the inside of this booklet.

2. Use a computer and headsets to record your conversation with a family member. Follow the directions inside this booklet. (We're here to help!)

3. Your recording will be ready for you within a week!

Finally, how can we deliver this to you?

Name of student _____

Grade/Class _____

Computer Station _____

How would you like to receive your copy of this interview? (Please choose one.)

o E-mail – must be able to accommodate attachments of 5 – 10MB

   (send to: _____)

o CD (will be sent home with the student when it is ready)

o Posting on the school Web site

If you enjoyed this project, you might like to learn about the StoryCorps project.

StoryCorps is a national recording project that travels throughout the U.S., bringing family members together and using professional recording equipment to gather their stories. Many of those recordings are heard on National Public Radio. You can learn more about StoryCorps and visit its audio archives at http://storycorps.net .

1. Double-click on the Audacity icon (a pair of blue headphones) on the Desktop. That will open the recording software.

2. Set your papers down on the table. (If you hold them in your hand, they will make noise).

3. Put on the headset. Make sure the mouthpiece is about 1" away from your mouth.

4. Now push the RECORD button (with a red dot in it) at the top of the screen. You will see blue sound waves going up and down as you talk. Your sound waves should fill up about half of the space. If the sound waves are too small, move the microphone closer to your mouth or speak up. If the sound waves are too large, move the microphone farther away from your face.

5. When you are done, click the STOP button (orangish square in it). If you want to play it back, press the REWIND button (2 blue arrows pointing left).

6. Ask an Oral History helper to come over and turn your file into mp3 format, the kind of file that can be heard on the Web or burned to CD. They will help you fill out the back page. **You're all done!**

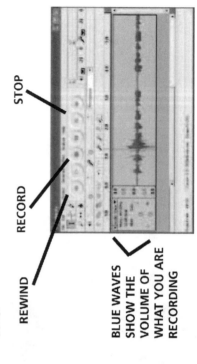

REWIND RECORD STOP

BLUE WAVES
SHOW THE
VOLUME OF
WHAT YOU ARE
RECORDING

First, plan your interview.

Questions for a Student to Ask an Adult:

Start by saying, "Hi, I'm (first name only). Today's date is _____. I'm here with my _____ to talk about what life was like when he/she was in elementary/middle/high school."

1. Who was your best friend when you were my age? What kinds of things did you do together? *Or write your own question here:*

2. What did you like about school? What did you dislike? *Or write your own question here:*

3. It's almost Spring Break. What did your family do during vacations? *Or write your own question here:*

When you are done, say, "Thank you."

Questions for an Adult to Ask a Student:

Start by saying, "Hi, I'm (first name only). Today's date is _____. I'm here with my _____ to talk about what life is like for him/her in elementary/middle/high school."

1. What do you like most about _____ School? *Or write your own question here:*

2. What is one great memory you have about our family? *Or write your own question here:*

3. What is one thing we do together as a family that you hope you will do with your own family some day? *Or write your own question here:*

When you are done, say, "Thank you."

Step Three: Record It

The day of the special school event, set up the computers in the hallway and put up signs guiding families to the podcasting stations. It may help to point out on the signs that the activity is free (especially if the stations are set up right outside of the book fair or another fundraising event). Have pencils located at each station.

As families come forward, guide them to a computer, open the software for them, and orient them to the brochure and the software. Encourage them to make a test recording and to look for sound waves that fill up about half of the available space. Then step away, saying that you are here if they need help and will return at the end to save and export the file for them.

As families wrap up their interviews, talk through the back page of the brochure with them. Depending on the size and popularity of the oral history station, you may choose to give them one option for receiving their podcast (e.g., CD or online link or e-mail) or multiple options. If there is not a long line, export the podcast directly to mp3 and e-mail, burn, or post it online right away. If there is a line waiting for the computer, export the file directly to mp3 and store it on the Desktop. Then take the brochure from the parent, notating the computer station on the back. Keep the brochures to double-check your work when you distribute the files later.

Step Four: Edit It

In general, this stage can be skipped for these family-created projects. The most common thing to check for is volume imbalance between parent and child, in which one voice is much louder or quieter than the others. Try highlighting the out-of-balance sound waves and using EFFECT > AMPLIFY to adjust the sound levels. If the entire track feels too loud or too soft, use the volume adjuster to the left of the sound waves to tweak it louder or softer.

Step Five: Review It

This is a nonassessed project. However, as the podcasts are prepared for export and distribution, take a moment for personal reflection:

- Did you have adequate staffing?

- Should you repeat this event next year?

- Would more or fewer computer stations make the project more successful?

- Was the brochure user-friendly?

- Did people seem happy or reluctant to participate?

- What would entice more people to participate?

- How can you archive this year's projects so that they can be shared again with families when their children are about to graduate or leave your school?

- How can background noise be reduced next year?

• Which administrators, department heads, or district leaders should receive a brief summary of the activity and a link to the podcasts that were posted online?

Step Six: Distribute It

In this author's experience, CDs are the most-requested format by parents. Parents often mention their plans to slip the CD into a student's memory book. Have plenty of CDs and paper CD cases ready. If time and finances permit, purchase adhesive CD labels and use the software that comes with those labels to create a generic label that can be customized with the family's name. Import the files into iTunes, create a playlist for each family's podcasts, and burn an audio CD. (Next year, try adding this year's oral history interview to next year's production, sharing with the families their accumulated conversation across the years.) Slip a small piece of paper into the CD sleeve that thanks parents for their participation: "Thank you for being a part of our school's oral history project. We hope you enjoy sharing this recording with your family. Come back next year for another chance to preserve family memories."

If e-mailing a file, send a note that says, "Thank you for being a part of our school's oral history project. Your family's project is attached. If you have any difficulties opening it, please e-mail us at _____ or call us at _____. We hope we will see you again next year for another oral history event!" Keep in mind that many e-mail accounts will reject files over 5MB in size. Some corporate e-mail filters reject all mp3 files as a matter of security, storage space, and prevention of music piracy. If this occurs, burn the file onto a CD and send it home with an explanation.

If a file is posted online, create a single page or blog entry that contains all of the oral history podcasts from that project, with a link to it from the school's home page. When a family's project is posted, send home a note that says something like, "Thank you for being a part of our school's oral history project. We have posted your family's podcast online at http://_____. We hope you'll join us again next year for another opportunity to preserve family memories."

■ CONCLUSION

Of all of the podcasting projects in this book, oral history podcasts can quickly become the most meaningful. They capture unrehearsed observations about world history and the world closer to home. They bring generations and families together. They illustrate the idea that technology, used correctly, can bind us more closely to those we love and respect.

Glossary

Analog audio recording: An audio recording recorded to reel-to-reel or cassette tape. Using special converter devices, analog audio recordings can be converted into digital audio recordings for use as podcasts.

Articulation: Movement of the mouth and jaw to make clear, accurate sounds.

Audacity: Free software for recording podcasts and music (http://audacity.sourceforge.net).

Audio loops: *See* Loops.

Bit depth: The amount of data processed for each piece of sound information. Too much bit depth can consume the processor speed of an older computer.

Blog: Short for Web log. An online journaling platform that facilitates comments by readers.

Blogger: Free blogging software by Google (http://www.blogger.com).

Browser: The software that lets you view and interact with Web sites. Examples are Internet Explorer by Microsoft, Safari for Macintosh, and Mozilla Firefox.

Categories: A way of classifying and sorting entries in a blog according to topic.

Chorus: A repeating refrain in a song.

Collective knowledge: Information about a topic that is generated by a variety of individuals contributing their individual knowledge.

Color commentary: The play-by-play spoken by sports announcers during a game.

Consumer advertising: Advertising that encourages the listener to buy a product.

Digital audio recording: An audio recording that is recorded as a data file. All podcasts are digital audio recordings.

Distribution of a podcast: The sharing of a podcast with others via e-mail, the Web, a CD, or an RSS feed.

Domain name: Part of the URL of a Web site. In the case of www.amazon.com, amazon.com is the domain name.

Embedded audio player: A plug-in that allows users to hear online audio on a Web page or blog entry, without leaving the blog for another page.

Energy: The "oomph" in our voices that communicates emotion and emphasis.

Enhanced podcast: A podcast that has accompanying visual images, similar to a small-screen PowerPoint™ presentation with audio. Most enhanced podcasts are made with GarageBand.

Feed: Packaging of blog, Web, or podcasting content so that it can be delivered to users via RSS. Built using XML programming language.

Feedburner: A Web site for creating feeds (http://www.feedburner.com).

File management: The process of organizing folders and documents.

File transfer protocol (FTP): A system that copies files from a computer to server space online. FTP is built into most Web authoring software. A free FTP option is Internet Explorer for Windows. When you set up a Web hosting account with your district or Web hosting company, they will give you the FTP address, as well as a username and password. Type it into the address bar of Internet Explorer (example: ftp://address.yourwebsite.com). A box will come up asking for the username and password, then your online files will appear. Move, copy, and rename online files using the same keystrokes used for file management on the Windows operating system. FTP is not currently built into the Firefox browser.

FTP: *See* File transfer protocol.

Gain: Amplification of audio input. For example, a TuneTalk attachment for a video iPod has an auto-gain feature that automatically boosts the amplification of the primary sound over ambient sound.

GarageBand: Apple's audio recording software. Ships free as part of the iLife software suite with the purchase of a new Macintosh computer. Requires the Macintosh OS10 operating system. Does not work with the Windows or Linux operating system.

Gigabyte (GB): 1,000 megabytes. A term used to measure the size of data.

GB: *See* Gigabyte.

Headset: A combination of a microphone and a set of headphones.

Input jack: The receptacle in the computer into which a microphone or headphone is plugged.

Interviewee: The person being interviewed.

Interviewer: The person asking the questions in an interview.

iPod: A digital audio player produced by Apple that, as of the writing of this book, is the market share leader. The sleek design and multiple accessories have made them a popular choice. Video iPods and the new iPod Nanos (as of fall 2006) can be partnered with an audio recording device such as a Belkin TuneTalk or a Griffin iTalk to make stereo-quality podcasts. View the current line of iPod products at http://www.apple.com/ipod.

Loops: Short audio clips containing rhythmic beats and/or melody. Loops can repeat over and over to make background music or a rap track. Loops are built into Apple's GarageBand software and can be downloaded from a variety of sites for use with Audacity.

Magazine show: A radio or television show that contains a variety of segments, with a host or hosts who introduce(s) each segment.

Megabyte (MB): A unit of measurement for file size. Average student podcasts are 5–10MB in size.

MB: *See* Megabyte.

Metadata: Data that describe other data. When exporting a podcast into mp3 format, the names given for the artist, title, album, etc., are the podcast's metadata.

Mnemonic device: A memory-aid device.

Mono: Audio that is recorded by a single microphone. Mono files record onto a single audio track in Audacity.

Moodle: Free, open source software used for online teaching and learning.

Mp3: Most common type of audio file available.

Mp3 player: A listening device that can play mp3 files. An iPod is an example of an mp3 player. Other common mp3 player brands are Sansa, Sony, Creative Zen, and iRiver.

Overarticulation: Overly careful, exaggerated pronunciation and speech via careful manipulation of the lips, teeth, and tongue.

Pitch: The register of the voice, a range from low to high.

Podcast: A digitally made audio recording that can be distributed easily and inexpensively, usually by posting it on the Web.

Plug-in: A Web tool that can be added on to enhance the functionality of another Web tool.

Public service announcement (PSAs): A radio or television ad aired by the station at little or no cost to the governmental or not-for-profit organization sponsoring the ad. PSAs focus on advocacy or changing behavior, not on selling products.

RSS or **RSS feed:** A string of Web coding based on XML language that allows blog, podcast, or Web page content to be automatically delivered to a subscriber.

Script: A document containing the words spoken by performers in a play. Radio play scripts also include sound effects.

Serial podcast: A podcast that is one of many in a series of similar format or theme, such as a weekly radio news broadcast.

Server: A computer that uses a network to deliver information to, or manage information for, users.

Server space: The amount of storage space on a server available to a registered user.

Sound effect: A nonspoken sound added to a radio play to help make the action more believable.

Soundscape: An audio collage of various environmental sounds.

Stereo: Audio that is recorded by two microphones. Stereo files record onto two audio tracks in Audacity.

TB: *See* Terabyte.

Teaser: A statement that gives a brief introduction to each story that will be covered in a radio broadcast.

Terabyte (TB): A term used to measure quantity of data. A terabyte equals 1,000 gigabytes.

Tone: *See* Energy.

Track: A song or audio segment on a CD. Also each individually recorded segment in audio editing software.

TypePad: A blogging site requiring a paid subscription.

Uploading: The process of putting a copy of a file on one's server. In almost all cases, uploading leaves a copy of the original file on the user's computer and places a copy on the server.

Verse: A "stanza" of a song. Most songs contain many verses, each of which has unique text.

Vocal variety: Manipulating the voice in different ways to change how it sounds.

Volume: Loudness or softness of sound.

Waveforms: The graphical representation of sound waves.

Web hosting provider: A company that registers domain names and hosts a subscriber's Web files on its server.

Web 2.0: An umbrella term describing the interactive, "read/write" Web.

Wiki: A Web site that can be edited by multiple users.

WordPress: A blogging software platform.

Bibliography

REFERENCES

Chen, Diane R. 2007. "Podcasting with No Dollars." *Practically Paradise* blog, *School Library Journal.* Available at http://www.schoollibraryjournal.com/blog/830000283/post/1790007579.html (accessed July 4, 2007).

Fontichiaro, Kristin. 2007. *Active Learning Through Drama, Podcasting, and Puppetry.* Westport, Conn.: Libraries Unlimited.

Isay, Dave. 2007. *Listening Is an Act of Love: A Celebration of American Lives from the StoryCorps Project.* New York: Penguin. ISBN 9781594201400.

"Jay Allison: 'This I Believe'." 2006. *Diane Rehm Show.* Available at http://www.wamu.org/programs/dr/06/11/16.php#12004 (accessed July 3, 2007).

Kelner, Lenore Blank, and Rosalind Flynn. 2006. *A Dramatic Approach to Reading Comprehension.* Portsmouth, N.H.: Heinemann. ISBN 0325007942.

Krathwohl, David. 2002, Autumn. "A Revision of Bloom's Taxonomy: An Overview—Benjamin S. Bloom, University of Chicago." *Theory into Practice.* Available at http://findarticles.com/p/articles/mi_m0NQM/is_4_41/ai_94872707/pg_1 (accessed July 4, 2007).

Nesbitt, Scott. 2007, February 25. *Tech Tip 114—Recording Skype Calls in Windows.* Available at http://www.geeks.com/techtips/2007/techtips-22feb07.htm (accessed June 1, 2007).

Vincent, Tony. 2005. *Radio WillowWeb: Guides to Help Make a Great Willowcast!* Available at http://learninginhand.com/podcasting/RadioWillowWeb.pdf (accessed July 4, 2007).

Warlick, David. 2006. Michigan Association for Media in Education Keynote Address, October 26.

Warlick, David. 2007. *Day One at TRLD. 2 Cents Worth Blog.* Available at http://davidwarlick.com/2cents/2007/02/01/day-one-at-trld/ (accessed July 4, 2007).

ADDITIONAL READING

A1 Free Sound Effects. *A1 Radio Sounds.* 2007. Available at http://www.a1freesoundeffects.com/radio.html (accessed July 4, 2007).

AIMS Multimedia. *Part 5: Readers Theatre: Historical Fiction.* UnitedStreaming, 2005. Available at http://www.unitedstreaming.com (accessed July 4, 2007).

Apple Inc. *Podcaster Tech Specs.* 2007. Available at http://www.apple.com/itunes/store/podcaststechspecs.html (accessed July 4, 2007).

Audacity Reference. Available at http://audacity.sourceforge.net/onlinehelp-1.2/ reference.html (accessed July 4, 2007).

Audacity Wiki Home Page. Available at http://audacityteam.org/wiki (accessed July 4, 2007).

Avi. *Nothing But the Truth: A Dcoumentary Novel.* New York: Orchard Books, 1991. ISBN 0531059596.

Beverly Media Center. Blog. *5th Grade Western Expansion Projects Here!* Available at http://beverlymedia.edublogs.org/2007/05/29/5th-grade-western-expansion-projects-here (accessed July 4, 2007).

Dahl, Roald. *Charlie and the Chocolate Factory.* New York: Knopf, 1973, 1964. ISBN 0394810112.

Deubel, Patricia. "Podcasts: Improving Quality and Accessibility." *T.H.E. Journal,* (June 2007). Available at http://www.thejournal.com/articles/20818 (accessed July 4, 2007).

———. "Podcasts: Where's the Learning?" *T.H.E. Journal* (June 2007). Available at http://www.thejournal.com/articles/20764 (accessed July 4, 2007).

Downs CE Primary School. *The Downs FM.* 2007. Available at http://www.downsfm.com (accessed July 4, 2007).

Fontichiaro, Kristin. "Podcasting 101." *School Library Media Activities Monthly* 23, no. 7 (March 2007), 23.

Hawthorne, Nathaniel. *The Scarlet Letter.* Clayton, DE: Prestwick House, 2005. ISBN 978-1580495950.

Keane, Nancy. *Nancy Keane's Children's Literature Webpage.* Available at http://www.nancykeane.com (accessed October 29, 2007).

Lee, Harper. *To Kill a Mockingbird.* New York: Harper Perennial Classics, 2006. ISBN 978-0061120084.

Library of Congress American Folklife Center. Veterans History Project. Available at http://www.loc.gov/vets (accessed July 4, 2007).

Lisagor, Kimberly. "Don't Leave Home Without It: iPods for Tourists." *USA Weekend,* June 8–10, 2007. Available at http://www.usaweekend.com/07_issues/070610/070610travelsmart.html (accessed July 4, 2007).

Longfellow Middle School. *Coulee Kids' Podcast.* Available at http://www.sdlax.net/longfellow/sc/ck/index.htm (accessed July 3, 2007).

Magnatune Web site. Available at http://www.magnatune.com (accessed July 3, 2007).

Nuance Communications. *Dragon Naturally Speaking.* 2007. Available at http://www.nuance.com/naturallyspeaking/ (accessed July 1, 2007)

Opp-Beckman, Leslie. *Pizzaz! Tongue Twisters.* 2004. Available at http://darkwing.uoregon.edu/~leslieob/twisters.html (accessed July 4, 2007).

Panic, Inc. *Transmit3.* Available at http://www.panic.com/transmit. (accessed July 4, 2007)

Plank Road Publishing. Available at http://www.musick8.com (accessed July 4, 2007).

Prairie Home Companion with Garrison Keillor. Available at http://prairiehome.publicradio.org (accessed July 4, 2007).

Richardson, Will. *Blogs, Wikis, Podcasts, and Other Powerful Web Tools for Classrooms.* Thousand Oaks, Calif.: Corwin Press, 2006. ISBN 9781412927673.

————.*Weblogg-ed.* Available at http://www.weblogg-ed.com (accessed July 4, 2007).

Shakespeare, William. *The Tragedy of Julius Caesar.* Edited by Barbara A. Mowat and Paul Werstein. New York: Washington Square Press, 1992. ISBN 9780671722715.

Staley, C.T. 2003. *Tongue Twister Database.* Available at http://www.geocities.com/athens/8136/tonguetwisters.html (accessed July 4, 2007).

Stanford University Libraries. *Copyright and Fair Use.* Available at http://fairuse.stanford.edu/Copyright_and_Fair_Use_Overview/chapter9/index.html (accessed July 4, 2007).

StoryCorps. Available at http://www.storycorps.net (accessed July 4, 2007).

This I Believe. *This I Believe Essay-Writing Instructions.* Available at http://www.thisibelieve.org/essaywritingtips.html (accessed July 3, 2007).

Tool Factory. *Tool Factory Podcasting.* Available at http://www.toolfactory.com/products/page?id=2121 (accessed July 1, 2007).

Tutorials—Audacity Wiki. Available at http://audacityteam.org/wiki/index.php?title=Tutorials (accessed July 4, 2007).

Willowdale Elementary School. *Radio WillowWeb.* Available at http://www.mpsomaha.org/willow/radio (accessed July 4, 2007).

Wordsmith. *Internet Anagram Server.* Available at http://wordsmith.org/anagram (accessed July 4, 2007).

Yale University Library. Fortunoff Video Archive for Holocaust Testimonies of Yale University Library. Available at http://www.library.yale.edu/testimonies (accessed July 4, 2007).

Index

Accreditation, 7
Acid Music Studio (Sony), 21, 113
Activity instructions, as podcasting lesson, 67
Adjusting volume, 117
Administrative support, 58
Administrators, 45
Adult-created projects, 99
Advanced Placement (AP), 12, 100
    as podcasting lesson, 67
Advertisements, 87–95
    consumer, 87
    as podcasting lesson, 68
    in radio broadcast project, 119
    types of, 87–88
Afghanistan, war in, in oral history project, 142
Aggregators, 6, 43. *See also* Bloglines; Google
    Reader; RSS feeds
Allison, Jay, 78
All-Night Party, 142
Amazon.com, 3–4
American Folklife Center, 84, 141
American Legion, 143
Amplifying sounds, 138
Anagrams, 57
Analog, 155
Ancient civilizations, 98
Ancient Greece, 120
Animal reports, as podcasting lesson, 68
Announcements, as podcasting lesson, 68
Anonymity, 57
A1 Sound Effects, 137
Apple, 7, 113, 120, 156
Apple Loops, 125. *See also* Loops
Appomattox, 131
Architecture, 12
Aristotle, 120
Art museums, 97

Art show tours, 97. *See also* Audio tours
    as podcasting lesson, 68
Articulation, 30, 155
Artist statements, as podcasting lesson, 68
Assessment, oral, as podcasting lesson, 68
Athletic director, 63
Audacity,15, 20, 33–34, 62, 125, 137, 155, 156
    downloading of, 33
    instructions for using, 37, 38, 152
    maximizing efficiency of, 34
    recording with, 36–39
Audacity toolbar, 38
Audio CD, 12
Audio loops, 20, 21, 155. *See also* Loops
Audio tours, 12, 20–21, 72, 84, 97–109
    as podcasting lesson, 68
Author/illustrator interviews, as podcasting
    lesson, 69
Avery labels, 47
Avi, 89
Avid, 18

Babbitt, Natalie, 121
Background music, removing extra, 117
Balancing volume, 117
Battle of the Books, 7, 22
Belkin, 23, 156
Beverly Media Center blog, 5, 131
Biographical sketch, as podcasting lesson, 69
Bit depth, 34, 155
Blackboard, 67
Blogger, 4, 5, 155
Bloglines, 6, 52
Blogs that talk, as podcasting lesson, 69
Blogs, 3–6, 7, 52, 67, 155
Bloom, Harold, 130
Bloom's Taxonomy, 130

Blue Mic, 19

Bluetooth, 26

Board of Education meetings, as podcasting
    lesson, 69

Bodies of water (in mnemonic rap projects), 112

Booktalks, 45
    in advertising project, 89
    as podcasting lesson, 69

Boston, 100

Boston Tea Party, 76

Brainstorming, 104, 115, 146

Branches of government (in mnemonic rap
    projects), 112

Breathing, 30

Broadcasts. *See* Radio broadcasts

Browser, 155

Buffalo Soldiers, 131

Business class, as podcasting lesson, 70

Caesar, 78

Calculus, 11

Califone, xiii

Call-in advice, in radio broadcast project, 119

Cassette recorders, xiii, 15

Categories, defined, 155

CD release parties, 47

CDs, 12, 37, 72, 81, 98, 118, 154

Cell phones, 104
    for podcasting. *See* Podcasting: with cell
        phones

Challenger explosion, in oral history project,
    142

Characters in literature, as podcasting lesson, 70.
    See also Literature

Chemistry class, 23, 44

Child safety seats, in PSA project, 87, 89

Chocolate phone by LG, 26, 100

Chorus, 113, 115, 155

Circulation policies, 57

Civics, 11

Civil War, 99, 131

Class presentations, as podcasting lesson, 70

Classroom procedures, in mnemonic raps, 111

Cleaning of equipment, 57–58

Clubs at school, in advertising project, 88

Collective knowledge, 6, 155

College Board, 67

Colonial Williamsburg, 99

Color commentary, 155

Community tree, 72

Conference calls, 22

Conferences, podcasting and, 7, 70

Conferencing with students, 138

Consumer advertisements, 155

Content management systems (CMS), 48, 50

Continents of the world (in mnemonic rap
    projects), 112

Cooking show, 74

Coolee Web, 120

Counselor/counseling program, 63
    as podcasting lesson, 70

CPR, 73

Creative Commons, 113, 118, 125

Creative Zen, 157
    Vision M, 24–25

Critiquing, 126

Current events podcasts, 119, 120

Curriculum, 15

Daily message to class, 71

Debate, as podcasting lesson, 71

Declaration of Independence, signing of, 129

Delicious, 113

Department of Homeland Security advice, in
    PSA project, 88

Dialogue, 134

Diane Rehm Show, The, 78

Diary of Anne Frank, The, 76

Dictation, 83

Differentiation, 97

Digital audio, 155

Digital voice recorders, 11, 25–26, 83

Disaster preparedness, in PSA project, 90

Discussion boards, 55

Distractions, minimizing, 148

Distribution. *See* Podcasts: distribution of

Domain name, 155

DownsFM, 120

Dragon Naturally Speaking, 25

Dramatic monologues, as podcasting lesson, 71

Dress code, in advertising project, 88

Driving and thinking, as podcasting lesson, 71

Driving tour, 12, 98–99. *See also* Audio tours

Drop Everything and Read (DEAR), 63

Echo, 138

Editing, 39

Editorials, 119, 120

Edublogs.org, 5, 52

Elmo (character on *Sesame Street),* 31

E-mail, 55

Embedded audio player, 155

Energy, 32, 155

English as a Second Language (ESL), as
    podcasting lesson, 71

English Language Learners (ELL), as podcasting
    lesson, 71

Enhanced podcast, 156

Enrichment, 63

Environmental center, as podcasting lesson, 71

Equipment cleaning. *See* Cleaning of equipment

Equipment setup and testing, 148

ESLblogs.org, 5

Essay, personal, 78

Evaluation rubrics, 91, 102, 114, 123, 132, 144

Exchanges with other classes, as podcasting
    lesson, 71

Exemplar, as podcasting lesson, 72

eXit interviews, as podcasting lesson, 85

Fading out sound, 117

Fairy tales, 11
    as podcasting lesson, 72

Family tree, as podcasting lesson, 72

Fantasy books, in advertising project, 89

Feedback, 55–56, 126

Feedburner, 156

Feeds, 120. *See also* RSS feeds

Field trip audio tours, 23, 99. *See also* Audio tours
    in advertising project, 88
    as podcasting lesson, 72

File management, 50, 156

File transfer protocol (FTP), 49, 156

Fire safety, in PSA project, 88, 89

Firefighters, in PSA project, 89

Five senses, 85

Fluency, 73

Fluency, reading, 79

Folktales, 5
    as podcasting lesson, 72

"Food Pyramid," 118
    in PSA project, 90

Ford, Henry, in advertising project, 89

Foreign language, 5
    in podcasting lesson, 72–73
    uses for podcasting, 23

Fortunoff Video Archive of Holocaust
    Testimonies, 141

Gabcast.com, 15, 26, 100, 104

Gain, 156

Gallery tours, 8. *See also* Audio tours

GarageBand software, 13, 20, 113, 120, 125,
    137, 156

Gcast.com, 15, 26, 100, 104

Genre studies, in radio plays, 129

Geocities, 3

Gettysburg Address, 131

Gigabyte (GB), 156

Globat.com, 50

GoDaddy.com, 50

Google, 4, 155

Google Reader, 6

GooglePages, 49

Graduation ceremonies, as podcasting lesson, 73

Graduation memories, as podcasting lesson, 73

Grammar, in advertising project, 89

Green Hornet, The, 129

Griffin, 24, 156

Gunshots, 137

Hamlet, 76

Hawthorne, Nathaniel, 89

Headsets, 17, 156

Health class, as podcasting lesson, 73

Health screenings, in PSA project, 88

Historical events, 112
    in radio plays, 129

Historical fiction, 130
    as podcasting lesson, 74
    in radio play, 130

Historical radio broadcasts, 120–121

History, as podcasting lesson, 74

Holocaust studies, 141, 145. *See also* Oral
    history: interviews
    as podcasting lesson, 74

Home economics, 74

Homework, as podcasting lesson, 74

HotRecorder, 22

Howe, James, 89
Human Resources department (HR), 70
Humanities, 5
Hypertext markup language (HTML), 3

iMovie, 21
Individualized education plans (IEPs), 11, 83
Input jack, 156
In-service, 58
Instructions for activities, 44, 67
Instrumental music, 78
Insurance, 26
Internet Explorer, 6, 155
Interviewee, slecting, 143, 145
Interviewer, 145
Interviews, 8, 119
    about the research process, 80
    author and illustrator, 69
    conclusions to, 147
    conducting, 148–149
    distributing, 149
    editing, 149
    with experts, 74
    in-studio, in radio broadcast project, 119
    introductions to, 147
    job, 70
    on-the-scene, in radio broadcast project, 119
    as podcasting lesson, 74
    questions for, developing, 145, 147
    reviewing, 149
    with veterans, 84
    when exiting class, 85
Introspection, as podcasting lesson, 74. *See also*
    Journaling; Reflection
Inventions, in advertising project, 89
iPodder, 43
iPods, 7, 11, 13, 23–24, 37, 43, 72, 100, 156
Iraq war, in oral history project, 142
iRiver, 157
iTalk Pro, 24, 156
iTunes, 11, 12, 24, 43, 52, 120
Iwo Jima, 76, 78

Jazz riffs, as podcasting lesson, 75. *See also*
    Music
Jingle, 92
Job interviews, 70

Journaling, as podcasting lesson, 75
Journalism, 119
Julius Caesar, 76, 78, 121

Keane, Nancy, 69
Keillor, Garrison, 137
Kennedy, John F., in oral history project, 142
Kinesthetic activities, as podcasting lesson, 75.
    See also Physical education
Korean War, in oral history project, 142
King, Martin Luther, Jr., in oral history project,
    142

Lab observations, as podcasting lesson, 75. *See
    also* Science
Lab safety, in advertising project, 90
LAME converter, 33
Language arts, xiv, 44. *See also* Literature
Language lab, as podcasting lesson, 75. *See also*
    Foreign language
Lanyard, 83
Learnerblogs.org, 5
Lee, Harper, 121
LG Chocolate phone, 26, 100
Library media center, 45
    orientation, as podcasting lesson, 75
Library of Congress, 84, 141, 145
Library orientations, xiv
Limited English Proficiency (LEP), 71
Lincoln, Abraham, 131
Listening kiosks, 43–44
Listening Is an Act of Love, 143
Literature, 121
    in advertising project, 89–90
    as podcasting lesson, 75–76
    in radio plays, 130
Little Orphan Annie, 129
Little Rock Central High School, integration of,
    78
Local history, in oral history project, 142
Local history tours. *See* Audio tours
Logitech, 19
Loops, 113, 125, 156

Magazine show, 119, 156
Magnatune.com, 125
Marketing class, 70

Massaging muscles, 29
Math facts, as podcasting lesson, 76
Math quiz, as podcasting lesson, 76
Media centers
    orientation, 75, 99
    uses for podcasting in, 5
Megabyte (MB), 156
Memphis Inter-Faith Association, 98
Metadata, 40, 157
Meter toolbar, 34
Microphones, 19–20, 113
Microsoft Outlook, 6
Misfits, The, 89
Mix-It-Up Day, 23
Mnemonic device, 111, 157
Mnemonic raps, 111–121
    as podcasting lesson, 76
Mnemonic rhyme/poem, 76
Mono, 157
Monologue, as podcasting lesson, 71, 76
Moodle, 67, 157
Mozilla Firefox, 6, 155
mp3
    format, 10, 24, 25, 37, 45, 157
    players, 11, 14, 23–25, 72, 97, 157
Multiplication tables, 76
    in mnemonic raps, 111
Music, 44–45
    as podcasting lesson, 77
Mystery classroom visitor, as podcasting lesson, 77
Mystery guest, as podcasting lesson, 68, 77

Narrator, 134
National Public Radio, 15, 78, 141
Nature walk. *See* Environmental center
News broadcast, 74
News broadcast. *See* Radio broadcasts
News show. *See* Radio broadcasts
Newsletter, as podcasting lesson, 77
Nicknames, 56–57
Noise, minimizing, 148
Nothing but the Truth, 89
Number/letter recognition, 45
Nutrition, in advertising project, 90

Old Faithful, 104
"Ol' Man River," 31

Olympic Games, in oral history project, 142
Olympus, 25–26, 83, 100
Omaha Public Schools, 122
"On the scene" recording, 125
Online experience, in oral history project, 142
Oral assessment, 68
Oral history
    brochure, 151–152
    events at school, 150–154
    interviews, 11, 72, 82, 84
    projects, 77, 141–154
    station, 150, 153–154
Oregon Trail, 98
Overarticulation, 30, 157

Paralympics, in oral history project, 142
Parent involvement, 61
Parent permission, 58–60
Parent–Teacher Associations/Organizations, as podcasting lesson, 77
Parent–teacher conferences, 44
    as podcasting lesson, 78
Park tour, 99
PBWiki.com, 6
Pen pals, 72
Periodic Table (in mnemonic rap projects), 112
Permission slip, 60, 83, 145
Personal essay, as podcasting lesson, 78
Physical education, 44, 118
    in advertising project, 90
    as podcasting lesson, 78
Picasa software, 4
Pitch, 31, 157
Planets (in mnemonic rap projects), 112
Plank Road Publishing, 113
Planning sheets, 124
Play-by-play, 82, 155
    variation, as podcasting lesson, 78
Playing tests, as podcasting lesson, 78
Plays, scenes from, in radio play, 130
Plosives, 17
Plug-in, 157
Podbean.com, 49
Podcasting
    with cell phones, 26
    definition of, xiii, 7
    distribution of, 138

Podcasting (*Cont.*)
  equipment, 17–32
  genres, 62
  myths, 13–15
  launching, 55–64
  policies and procedures for, 56–57
  practical procedures for, 57–58
  setting up for, 35
  software, 20–32
  steps in process, 8–12
  with stuffed animal, 80
  with voice mail, 26
Podcasting at School wiki, xiii, xiv, 7, 67
Podcasting clubs, 11, 61–64
Podcasting lessons, suggested, 67–85
Podcasts
  burning to CD, 46–47
  definition of, 157
  distribution of, 7, 11, 43–53, 100–101, 128,
    118–119, 149, 154
  editing, 108
  e-mailing as attachments, 45
  exporting of, 10, 40
  recording a, 10, 33–36, 138
  saving, 40
  size of, 47–48
  uploading, 47–53
PodOMatic.com, 49
Poetry, as podcasting lesson, 78
Police officers, in PSA project, 89
Policies and procedures, 56–57
Portable recording devices, 22–26
PowerGramo, 22
PowerPoint, 20, 156
Prairie Home Companion, A, 137
Prepositions (in mnemonic rap projects), 112
Presidents (in mnemonic rap projects), 112
Primary Rap Builder, 113, 115
Principals, 5
  message, as podcasting lesson, 79
Professional development, as podcasting lesson, 79
Professional learning communities, 55
Project maps, 103
Project partners, 101
Public service announcements (PSAs), 8, 73,
  87–88, 157
  as podcasting lesson, 79

Qualitative research, as podcasting lesson, 79
Question Generator, 147
QuickTime Pro, 21
Quinceañera, in oral history project, 142

Radio broadcasts, 7, 8, 119–128
  planning, 121–122
  as podcasting lesson, 79
Radio plays, 74, 129–139
  historical fiction, 130–139
  planning, 131–132
Radio Shack, 19
Radio show. *See* Radio broadcasts
Radio WillowWeb, 120, 128
Rap tracks, 113
Raps, 111–121
  planning, 112–113
  as podcasting lesson, 79
Reading fluency, as podcasting lesson, 80
Reading specialist, 63
Recording "on the scene," 125
Reflection, 71, 126–127, 138, 153
Rehearsals, as podcasting lesson, 80
Rehm, Diane, 78
Relaxation techniques, 29
Reports, animal, 68
Research process interviews, as podcasting
  lesson, 80
Research, qualitative, as podcasting lesson, 79
Reviews, in radio broadcast project, 119
Rhyming patterns, 115
Rhythm instruments, 137
Rites of passage, as podcasting lesson, 80
Rock the Vote, in PSA project, 89
Romeo and Juliet, 130
Royalties, 113
Royalty-free loops, 113
RSS feeds, 6, 11, 43, 83, 156, 157
Rubrics, evaluation. *See* Evaluation rubrics

Safari browser, 155
Sandwiching technique, 126
Sanitizing wipes, 17
Sansa, 157
Scarlet Letter, The, 89
School handbook and acceptable language, 112
School libraries. *See* Media centers

School life, in advertising project, 89
School motto, as podcasting lesson, 81
School nurse, 63
School policies, in advertising project, 88
School prayer, as podcasting lesson, 81
School song, as podcasting lesson, 81
School tours, 97. *See also* Audio tours
    as podcasting lesson, 81
Science, xiv,
    in advertising project, 90
Science experiments
    in mnemonic raps, 111
    as podcasting lesson, 81
Science lab safety tour, 99. *See also* Science
Screensaver, 34
Scripts, 35, 157
    marking to improve vocal performance, 32
    sample of, 136, 137
    writing, 134
Seat belts, in PSA project, 87, 89
Seedwiki, 6
Self-evaluation, 135
Senior centers, 143
September 11, 2001 (oral history project event), 142
Serial podcasts, 11, 157
Server space, 47–52, 157
Servers, 47, 157
Sesame Street, 31
Shakespeare, William, 121, 130
    in advertising project, 88
    as podcasting lesson, 76, 81
Shoulders, loosening, 30
Show and tell, as podcasting lesson, 81
Singing telegrams, as podcasting lesson, 81
60 Minutes, 15
Skype, 22
Slang, use of in mnemonic rap projects, 112
Snowball microphone, 19, 72, 117
Social studies, xiv, 44, 63
    in advertising project, 89
Social worker/social work, 23
Soliloquoy, as podcasting lesson, 81
Sony, 21, 113, 157
Sony Acid Music Studio. *See* Acid Music Studio
    (Sony)
Sound effects, 37, 39,129, 134, 137, 138, 157
Sound engineer, 138

Sound levels, 36
Soundscapes, 99, 157
South America, 5
Space flight, in oral history project, 142
Special education, 64. *See also* Individualized
        education plans
    students, as podcasting lesson, 83
Speech therapy/speech therapists, 12, 45
    as podcasting lesson, 81
Speed of speech, 31
Spelling tests, 11, 44
    as podcasting lesson, 82
Sponge activities, 44
    as podcasting lesson, 82
Sports play-by-play, as podcasting lesson, 82
Sports updates, in radio broadcast project, 119
Sputnik, in oral history project, 142
State assessments, 15
State capitals (in mnemonic rap projects), 112
States (in mnemonic rap projects), 112
Stereo, 157
Story dictation, as podcasting lesson, 82
Story structure, as podcasting lesson, 82
StoryCorps, 141, 143, 148. *See also* Oral history:
        interviews
    as podcasting lesson, 82
StoryCorps Question Generator, 147, 150
Streetwise language, use of in mnemonic rap
        projects, 112
Student fluency, 45, 73
Student portfolios, 47
Student privacy, 15, 56–57
Student-created projects, 97–99
Students with special needs, as podcasting
        lesson, 83
Studio recording, 125
Summer reading, as podcasting lesson, 83
Super Bowl, in oral history project, 142
Superintendents, 5
Switch software, 26
Switchpod, 49

Talking blogs. *See* Blogs that talk
Talkr, 69, 79
Teaser, 122, 157
Tech tips, as podcasting lesson, 83
Terabyte (TB), 157

This I Believe, as podcasting lesson, 78
Time capsule, as podcasting lesson, 84
To Kill a Mockingbird, 121
Tone, 32, 157
Tongue twisters, 30–31
Tool Factory Podcasting, 21, 25, 137
Toolbar, 34
Tours. *See also* Audio tours
    of historical neighborhoods, 98
    of local attractions, 97
    as podcasting lesson, 84
Track, 157
Traffic
    safety, in PSA project, 88, 89
    updates, in radio broadcast project, 119
Trivia questions, in radio broadcast project, 119
Tuck Everlasting, 121
TuneTalk, 23, 72, 100, 117, 156
TypePad.com, 4, 157

United Kingdom, 120
Uploading, 47–52, 158
U.S. history, 100
USB microphone. *See* Microphones
Use of language in mnemonic rap projects, 112

Verse, 113, 115, 158
Veterans History Project, 84, 141, 143, 145, 147,
    148, 149
Veterans' interviews, as podcasting lesson, 84
Veterans of Foreign Wars, 143
Victory Gardens, 120
    in advertising project, 89
Vietnam War, in oral history project, 142
Vincent, Tony, 123
Vocal variety, 31–32, 158
Vocal warm-ups and exercises, 9, 29–32,
    as podcasting lesson, 84
Voice mail, 15
    podcasts. *See* Podcasting: with voice mail
Volume, 31, 158
    adjustment, 115
    balancing, in Audacity, 117

Walker, Madam C. J., in advertising project, 89
Walking tour, as podcasting lesson, 84. *See also*
    Audio tours
Warm-ups, 115
Washington, George, 76, 129
Washington crossing the Delaware, 76, 129
WAV files, 24, 25, 26
Waveforms, 34, 158
Weather forecasts, in radio broadcast project, 119
Web hosting, 48
    provider, 158
Web links, 51
Web space, 48
Web 2.0, xiv, 3–12, 158
Welcome to class as podcasting lesson, 84
Wikipedia, 6–7
Wikis, 3, 6–7, 158
Wikis, 55
Wikispaces, 6
WMA format, 26
WordPress, 4–5, 52, 158
World Series, in oral history project, 142
World War I, in oral history project, 141
World War II
    in advertising project, 89
    in Holocaust studies, 74
    in oral history project, 142
    in radio broadcast project, 120
Wright Brothers, in advertising project, 89
Writer's workshop, as podcasting lesson, 84
Writing curriculum, in advertising project, 89
Writing directions, as podcasting lesson, 85
Writing process, in mnemonic raps, 111

XML, 156

Y adapter, 18–19, 35, 151
Yahoo, 3
Yale University Library, 141
Yellowstone National Park, 104
Yoga poses, 85

Zion National Park, 100
Zoo, 72, 99
    as podcasting lesson, 85